THE EVERYTHING.
GLUTEN-FREE
BREAKFAST AND BRUNCH
COOKBOOK

Dear Reader,

Eating a gluten-free diet may seem challenging, especially at first when you are just learning what is and is not safe to eat. Breakfast can be particularly daunting because so many popular breakfast foods are full of gluten . . . waffles, pancakes, French toast, muffins, bagels. You may feel like you will never enjoy breakfast again! But I promise that you will.

When I first went gluten-free, I think I ate eggs for breakfast every day for a month. Then I discovered the plethora of gluten-free products in the marketplace. Buying gluten-free breakfast foods can get pricey, so I learned how to cook my favorite breakfast recipes without gluten right in my own kitchen. This book includes many of my own recipes as well as those that others have submitted. Some of the recipes in this book are naturally gluten-free, and others are a makeover of your favorite glutinous breakfast dishes, but all are safe for you to eat, and they're delicious.

With these 300 gluten-free breakfast options at your fingertips, you will be able to start your day on the right track and never feel deprived.

Jo-Lynne Shane

Welcome to the EVERYTHING® Series!

These handy, accessible books give you all you need to tackle a difficult project, gain a new hobby, comprehend a fascinating topic, prepare for an exam, or even brush up on something you learned back in school but have since forgotten.

You can choose to read an Everything® book from cover to cover or just pick out the information you want from our four useful boxes: e-questions, e-facts, e-alerts, and e-ssentials.

We give you everything you need to know on the subject, but throw in a lot of fun stuff along the way, too.

We now have more than 400 Everything® books in print, spanning such wide-ranging categories as weddings, pregnancy, cooking, music instruction, foreign language, crafts, pets, New Age, and so much more. When you're done reading them all, you can finally say you know Everything®!

QUESTION

Answers to common questions

FACT

Important snippets of information

ALERT

Urgent warnings

ESSENTIAL

Quick handy tips

PUBLISHER Karen Cooper

MANAGING EDITOR, EVERYTHING® SERIES Lisa Laing

COPY CHIEF Casey Ebert

ASSISTANT PRODUCTION EDITOR Alex Guarco

ACQUISITIONS EDITOR Eileen Mullan

ASSOCIATE DEVELOPMENT EDITOR Eileen Mullan

EVERYTHING® SERIES COVER DESIGNER Erin Alexander

THE
EVERYTHING®
GLUTEN-FREE
BREAKFAST AND BRUNCH
COOKBOOK

Jo-Lynne Shane

Avon, Massachusetts

This book is dedicated to those with celiac disease, gluten sensitivities, wheat allergies, and anyone seeking to remove gluten from their diets so they can live healthier, happier lives.

An Everything® Series Book.
Everything® and everything.com® are registered trademarks of F+W Media, Inc.

Published by
Adams Media, a division of F+W Media, Inc.
57 Littlefield Street, Avon, MA 02322. U.S.A.
www.adamsmedia.com

ISBN 10: 1-4405-8008-1
ISBN 13: 978-1-4405-8008-6
eISBN 10: 1-4405-8009-X
eISBN 13: 978-1-4405-8009-3

Printed in the United States of America.

10 9 8 7 6 5 4 3 2 1

Library of Congress Cataloging-in-Publication Data
Shane, Jo-Lynne.
The everything gluten-free breakfast and brunch cookbook / Jo-Lynne Shane
pages cm
Includes index.
ISBN-13: 978-1-4405-8008-6 (pb)
ISBN-10: 1-4405-8008-1 (pb)
ISBN-13: 978-1-4405-8009-3 (ebook)
ISBN-10: 1-4405-8009-X (ebook)
1. Gluten-free diet--Recipes. 2. Breakfasts.
3. Brunches. I. Title.
RM237.86.S52 2014
641.5'638—dc23
2014012060

Contains material adapted and abridged from *The Everything® Wheat-Free Diet Cookbook* by Lauren Kelly, CN, copyright © 2013 by F+W Media, Inc., ISBN 10: 1-4405-5680-6, ISBN 13: 978-1-4405-5680-7; *The Everything® Gluten-Free Cookbook* by Richard Marx and Nancy T. Maar, copyright © 2006 by F+W Media, Inc., ISBN 10: 1-59337-394-5, ISBN 13: 978-1-59337-394-8; *The Everything® Paleolithic Diet Cookbook* by Jodie Cohen and Gilaad Cohen, copyright © 2011 by F+W Media, Inc., ISBN 10: 1-4405-1206-X, ISBN 13: 978-1-4405-1206-3; *The Everything® Gluten-Free Slow Cooker Cookbook* by Carrie S. Forbes, copyright © 2012 by F+W Media, Inc., ISBN 10: 1-4405-3366-0, ISBN 13: 978-1-4405-3366-2; *The Everything® Paleolithic Diet Slow Cooker Cookbook* by Emily Dionne, MS, RD, LDN, CDDS, ACSM-HFS, copyright © 2013 by F+W Media, Inc., ISBN 10: 1-4405-5536-2, ISBN 13: 978-1-4405-5536-7; *The Everything® Green Smoothies Book* by Britt Brandon with Lorena Novak Bull, RD, copyright © 2011 by F+W Media, Inc., ISBN 10: 1-4405-2564-1, ISBN 13: 978-1-4405-2564-3.

Always follow safety and commonsense cooking protocol while using kitchen utensils, operating ovens and stoves, and handling uncooked food. If children are assisting in the preparation of any recipe, they should always be supervised by an adult.

Photographs by Jennifer L. Yandle.

Cover photos © Jennifer L. Yandle;
© StockFood/Food Image Source/Leatart, Brian;
© StockFood/Eising Studio - Food Photo & Video.

*This book is available at quantity discounts for bulk purchases.
For information, please call 1-800-289-0963.*

Contents

Acknowledgments

First and foremost, I want to thank my husband, Paul, for your patience during the cookbook writing (and baking) process. I couldn't have done it without your support. Thanks also to my children, David, Caroline, and Rebecca, for being such willing little taste testers. It's a tough job . . . or maybe not. I know you will miss having homemade donuts every weekend!

To all my neighbors and friends and faithful readers of my blog, *musingsofahouse wife.com*, I appreciate your support and encouragement throughout this entire process. I also want to thank all my friends and fellow bloggers who submitted recipes to this book and helped me reach my deadline just in the nick of time! I couldn't have done this without you. Finally, thanks to everyone at Adams Media, particularly my editor, Eileen, for bringing me this opportunity and for your guidance and support every step of the way.

Introduction

EVERYONE KNOWS THAT BREAKFAST is the most important meal of the day. The right breakfast can give you the energy and nutrition you need to start your morning off right and tackle whatever comes your way. But if you are living gluten-free, finding delicious and healthful breakfast and brunch foods can be tricky.

Contrary to popular belief, muffins, waffles, and doughnuts do not have to contain gluten to be tasty. Just because you have gluten intolerance, celiac disease, or are looking to live a gluten-free life doesn't mean you don't want to be able to eat your favorite breakfast and brunch foods. You just have to learn new ways to make them, and that's exactly what this book helps you do. You will find new recipes to try in addition to tips for making gluten-free versions of popular breakfast and brunch favorites.

The book is divided into popular categories for breakfast and brunch foods from pancakes and waffles to eggs, muffins, and more. It is intended to give you a wide sampling of common brunch and breakfast foods, so you never have to miss out again.

Gluten sensitivities can manifest in many different ways. Just because you test negative for celiac disease doesn't mean that you can't benefit from removing gluten from your diet. If you have inexplicable headaches, joint pain and stiffness, "foggy mind," or numbness in your legs, arms, or fingers, you could be reacting to gluten or other food triggers. Symptoms typically appear hours after gluten has been ingested, but sometimes not for a day or so. For those with gluten sensitivity, it is often a buildup of gluten in the body that causes problems, so sometimes it is hard to pinpoint the exact trigger. Often those who are sensitive to gluten find that they are also sensitive to other grains such as corn and rice, so the recipes in this cookbook use a variety of flours, and there are some grain-free options as well.

While most of the recipes in this cookbook contain common ingredients, you will need to purchase a few different types of gluten-free flours for some of the recipes. Most grocery stores carry a variety of gluten-free flours and other cooking ingredients, and you can also find a huge assortment online.

Living gluten-free can be a difficult undertaking. Let your friends know that you are living gluten-free, and see if they'd like to help you experiment with new gluten-free foods and recipes. There's no need to spend a ton of money on a fancy brunch at a popular restaurant when you can make healthy, mouthwatering gluten-free foods at home.

Lastly, it is important to have the support of family members as you seek to live a gluten-free lifestyle. These recipes are intended to be delicious options for those who must eat gluten-free as well as for their loved ones who share these meals. This book will show you how to live a healthy, gluten-free life and still enjoy the best breakfast and brunch foods available.

CHAPTER 1

Gluten-Free Basics

When starting on your gluten-free journey, breakfast can feel like the most challenging meal of the day. After all, breakfast foods like cereal, pancakes, muffins, and bagels may seem like the antithesis of gluten-free living, but with the variety of recipes in this book, you won't feel deprived. These recipes are all about showing you how to make your favorite breakfast foods gluten-free. Once you learn what you can and can't eat, and stock your kitchen with foods that are naturally gluten-free along with some tasty gluten-free alternatives, you will be well on your way to a healthy and happy gluten-free life. And yes, you *will* enjoy waffles again!

What Is Gluten?

Gluten is a protein found in wheat, barley, and rye. It is often present in breads, cakes, cookies, and pasta. Those are the obvious culprits, but gluten can be hidden in many processed foods as well, some of which may surprise you! For example, soy sauce, salad dressings, and beer can contain gluten. Many sauces and packets on the grocery store shelves contain gluten as well. You will soon become an expert label reader and be able to decipher food labels with the best of them, but there is a bit of a learning curve involved, so be patient at first and allow extra time for grocery shopping until you get the hang of it.

Celiac Disease and Gluten Intolerance

Gluten is not inherently unhealthy for the general population, but it is extremely harmful for people with celiac disease. Celiac disease is an autoimmune disorder that causes the body to attack the small intestine and prevents it from absorbing essential nutrients. Celiac disease is linked to iron deficiency and osteoporosis, and it can raise your risk of other diseases. Even if you have no outward symptoms of celiac disease, once you're diagnosed, it is imperative that you avoid gluten at all costs.

Unlike celiac disease, gluten intolerance is not an autoimmune condition, and consuming gluten does not damage the small intestine for these individuals. However, those with gluten intolerance may experience severe reactions to gluten including headaches, joint pain, skin rash, "foggy brain," and intestinal issues, to name a few. Often their symptoms are strikingly similar to those with celiac disease.

ALERT

It is very important *not* to remove gluten from your diet before you are tested for celiac disease. It's crucial for gluten to be in your system to get accurate results, so if you plan to be tested, hold off on the elimination diet until you have your test results back.

Celiac disease can be diagnosed with a blood test and biopsy through endoscopy. There are no tests to diagnose gluten intolerance. If you test negative for celiac and you still believe gluten to be the culprit of your complaints, the best way to diagnose a gluten intolerance is to remove gluten from your diet and see how you feel when it's reintroduced a few weeks later. Many people feel relief immediately upon removing gluten from their diets.

Basic Ingredients for a Gluten-Free Diet

When you start your gluten-free lifestyle, you will want to remove all gluten-containing products from your kitchen if at all possible. It's important to have a clean kitchen to avoid the risk of cross-contamination, but it also cuts down on unnecessary temptations.

If you're sharing a kitchen with gluten-consuming individuals, it's best to separate and label the gluten-free products so you can find them easily and avoid cross-contamination. While someone with gluten intolerance may not get sick from a few small crumbs of gluten, someone with celiac disease may become very ill from just a speck of gluten. And even if they don't feel the effects (some celiac sufferers do not) the gluten does damage to the small intestine just the same. For this reason, it is imperative that people with celiac disease avoid gluten at all costs.

What Can I Eat?

Eating gluten-free is not as difficult as it may seem at first, but it does take some planning and preparation. Start out by stocking up on food that is naturally gluten-free. Fortunately, many foods in their natural state are gluten-free. Here is a list to get you started:

- Fruits
- Vegetables
- Beef
- Chicken
- Fish
- Milk
- Hard Cheeses
- Yogurt
- Butter
- Eggs
- Beans
- Rice
- Nuts and seeds

Fresh and frozen fruits and vegetables are always gluten-free, unless they come with a seasoning packet or are submerged in some type of sauce. So are meats, milk, eggs, and most milk-based products such as sour cream and plain yogurt. Most aged cheeses such as Cheddar and Parmesan are safe, but blue cheeses and cheese spreads can be problematic. Again, this is assuming they have not been seasoned in any way. Rice and quinoa are gluten-free, and they can replace pasta in many dishes. Beware of rice mixes, which may contain gluten derivatives in their seasonings and preservatives.

In addition to foods that are naturally gluten-free, there are many gluten-free replacements for your favorite foods on the supermarket shelves. It takes some trial and error to find the ones that you like, but you will eventually find gluten-free versions of your old favorites. There is everything from cookies to crackers and chips to breads and cake available in gluten-free versions nowadays. The gluten-free food industry has come very far in the last ten years, so if you don't like the first product you try, try another until you find one that works for you.

How to Avoid Gluten

Gluten is not usually listed in the ingredients list on a food label. You will have to dig a little deeper to tell whether or not a food product contains gluten. Some foods are obvious. For starters, avoid all breads, cakes, crackers, cookies, and pastas made with flour from wheat, barley, or rye. Unfortunately, avoiding gluten doesn't end there. There are many innocent-looking foods that can harbor traces of gluten. For example, soy sauce, salad dressings, lunchmeats, and baking powder may (or may not) contain gluten. Who knew?

FACT

You may think that because you can't have gluten, you can't have flour. This is not necessarily true. There are many flours made from grains that are naturally gluten-free (such as rice, millet, buckwheat, and quinoa). It is just a matter of learning to use these new flours in your favorite recipes.

If you are new to gluten-free living, it's important to learn all the foods that can possibly contain gluten so you don't unknowingly get exposed.

Deciphering Labels

The more highly processed a food is, the more chance there is of it containing a source of gluten, so be on the lookout for any food products containing sauces, thickeners, and stabilizers.

Here is a list of words to watch out for on food labels. These are the words you do *not* want to see, because they indicate the presence of gluten:

- Barley
- Breading and bread stuffing
- Brewer's yeast
- Bulgur
- Durum (a type of wheat)
- Farro
- Graham flour
- Hydrolyzed wheat protein
- Kamut (a type of wheat)
- Malt, malt extract, malt syrup, malt flavoring, malt vinegar, malted milk
- Matzo, matzo meal
- Modified wheat starch
- Oatmeal, oat bran, oat flour, and whole oats (unless they are from pure, uncontaminated oats)
- Rye bread and flour
- Seitan (a meat-like food derived from wheat gluten, used in many vegetarian dishes)
- Semolina
- Spelt (a type of wheat also known as farro or dinkel)
- Triticale
- Wheat bran, wheat flour, wheat germ, or wheat starch

This list is not exhaustive, but it is a good place to start. You may want to print it out and carry it with you for a while until you get the hang of gluten-free living. When in doubt of a product, don't buy it before doing your research. It is better to be safe than sorry when it comes to gluten.

Many manufacturers are now putting "gluten-free" on their products, which is a helpful tool when you don't have the time to stand in the middle of a grocery aisle reading every ingredient on the back of a box. But keep in mind, a "gluten-free" label is not currently required by the FDA. Many foods are naturally gluten-free, so just because a product does not say "gluten-free" does not necessarily mean that it contains gluten.

FACT

Oats are technically gluten-free, but because of the way they are processed, most have been contaminated. The only way to be certain oats are gluten-free is to purchase those labeled "Certified Gluten Free," such as Bob's Red Mill. Some people who are sensitive to gluten also find they are sensitive to oats as well, so try them and see how you feel.

On the other hand, if a product does say "gluten-free" or "free of gluten" somewhere on the label, the manufacturer is accountable to the FDA for using the claim in a truthful manner, so it should be trustworthy. Still, it's never a bad idea to double-check with the manufacturer, especially if you are highly sensitive to the slightest trace of gluten in your food.

Make It at Home

When you have dietary restrictions, it is always less expensive (and sometimes less stressful!) to make your food at home. That is where this book comes in handy. Most recipes use common ingredients, but there are a few gluten-free staples you will want to purchase if you're planning to do much gluten-free baking.

A gluten-free all-purpose flour blend is indispensible in a gluten-free kitchen. Not only can you use it to make gluten-free baked goods, but it is helpful to have on hand for gravies and sauces that require a thickener. Not all gluten-free, all-purpose flour blends are the same, so you may want to experiment with a few. Bob's Red Mill is highly recommended. A gluten-free baking mix such as Pamela's Products Ultimate Baking and Pancake Mix (recommended) is also nice to have in your pantry and is used in several recipes in this book. Cornstarch is another option for thickening gravies and sauces, and you may also want to keep xanthan gum on hand.

QUESTION

What is xanthan gum?
Xanthan gum is a plant-based thickening and stabilizing agent that mimics the quality of gluten in gluten-free baking and helps breads and cakes have the spongy texture we have come to expect. It is helpful for gluten-free baking, but not absolutely necessary. Xanthan gum is a corn-based product, so if you have a sensitivity or an allergy to corn, you probably want to do without.

If you keep gluten-free bread in the freezer, then you can easily whip up some bread crumbs or make croutons if you need to. It also makes great toast, which can be a vehicle for all sorts of delicious toppings and salads. Think outside the box, and try new ways to use some of your old favorites.

There are many other flours that are great to have on hand, and some are used in the recipes in this cookbook, such as:

- Almond flour
- Brown rice flour
- Buckwheat flour
- Coconut flour
- Millet

- Oatmeal flour
- Potato flour
- Sorghum
- Tapioca starch
- White rice flour

QUESTION

How do I convert one of my regular recipes to make it gluten-free?
You can take almost any regular recipe for quick breads, muffins, waffles, or pancakes and substitute gluten-free all-purpose flour (Bob's Red Mill is recommended) plus a teaspoon of xanthan gum per cup of flour and get similar results.

You will want to experiment and see which flours you like best. Gluten-free baking is most successful when a combination of flours is used, which is why a gluten-free, all-purpose flour blend is nice to have. If you don't want to keep so many different flours in your pantry, an all-purpose flour blend can be substituted in most recipes. If the baking mix contains xanthan gum, there is no need to add more. However, if the baking mix does not contain xanthan gum, you will get better results if you add a teaspoon per cup of gluten-free flour. Again, this is optional if you are sensitive to corn.

Preventing Cross-Contamination

Depending on how sensitive you are to gluten, you may need to take extra precautions to avoid cross-contamination. The safest way to be assured you won't come in contact with gluten is to keep a gluten-free kitchen. If that's not possible, you will have to take extreme care that your foods not come in contact with the slightest bit of gluten.

Train all members of the household not to "double dip" when using peanut butter and condiments. Better yet, purchase two sets of condiments and keep a gluten-free and a regular version of each. Labels are your friends!

Some households even have two toaster ovens in order to keep the gluten-free foods separate from the regular. Make use of labels and carefully designate which foods are gluten-free and which are not, especially if you have children in the home.

Here are some basic rules to help avoid cross-contamination:

- Use separate cutting boards for gluten-free food prep.
- Purchase a second toaster for gluten-free foods only.
- Prepare gluten-free foods and meals on a clean counter or cutting board *before* preparing gluten-containing foods.
- Label gluten-free foods with stickers or markers.
- Wash all cooking pans and utensils thoroughly in hot, soapy water.
- Store gluten-free foods above gluten-containing foods in the pantry.
- Have a separate area for gluten-free condiments in the refrigerator, and purchase separate condiment jars that are labeled gluten-free.
- If in doubt, throw it out.

At first it's hard to remember to do all of these things, but they will soon become habits. In the meantime, it might be helpful to post small signs or notes around the kitchen to remind all members of the household of the new rules.

Dining Out

When dining out, it is extremely important to notify the wait staff of your gluten-free requirements, and don't be afraid to double-check when your food is delivered that you are getting a gluten-free meal. Cross-contamination is always a risk, but it's becoming quite common to find gluten-free menus and restaurant personnel who are well informed about the dangers of gluten for their celiac and gluten-sensitive customers. Be polite, but be sure to speak up and make your dietary needs known.

If your plate does arrive with bread or croutons or any other obvious source of gluten, send it back immediately and ask for a new meal. Be sure to state clearly that absolutely nothing with gluten can come in contact with your food. Not realizing the seriousness of cross-contamination, a server may be tempted to simply remove the croutons or the bread rather than making a new meal. To be safe, you can mark your plate in some way (douse it with ketchup, for example) so you can tell if the server removed the bread and brought back the same plate.

Be aware that eggs are often prepared on the same griddle as pancakes, and oftentimes pancake batter is added to scrambled eggs and omelets. It is important to be very specific with your server about your gluten-free needs and the dangers of cross-contamination, especially if you have celiac disease, because even the smallest bit of gluten can damage the small intestine and cause pain and discomfort.

Social Gatherings

Social gatherings present another set of challenges when avoiding gluten. Again, with adequate planning, you can still enjoy parties and get-togethers. If possible, let your host know of your dietary restrictions ahead of time, preferably before she plans the menu. Offer to bring a gluten-free dish or two to share. If you're not sure that there will be gluten-free food available at a social gathering, bring your own. If the occasion involves a buffet, consider asking your host if you can go first and fill your plate before cross-contamination can occur. Always be polite, but don't be afraid to speak up and let people know that you need to eat gluten-free. When you don't know the hosts or the party is too big to alert them ahead of time, it is always best to eat a light meal before you go. Don't ever arrive at a social situation hungry. Eat lightly before you go, and then be sure to have a snack in your purse to tide you over if you need to eat again before you get home.

Travel

The same is true when traveling. If you're taking a road trip, pack a cooler with plenty of snacks to keep you full until you get to your destination. If you're not sure there will be gluten-free food along the way, pack for your meals as well. Airports are still a bit behind the times when it comes to gluten-free fare, especially airplanes. You will want to arrive at the airport extra early and scope out the options. It's best to buy a meal in the airport and bring it with you on the plane since most airlines do not have a lot of gluten-free offerings. Pack snacks in your suitcase to have when you reach your destination if you don't know that adequate options will be provided there.

Health Benefits of Eating Gluten-Free

You may be surprised to find that gluten-free living has some unexpected health benefits. You may suddenly feel more clear-headed. If you struggle with joint pain and stiffness or headaches, you may find that those symptoms disappear with the gluten-free lifestyle. You will probably feel less bloated and gassy, and you may find you have more energy.

In our carb-heavy culture, gluten-free living forces you to eat more protein and vegetables and fewer carbs (although, don't worry, there are plenty of carbolicious recipes in this book if that's your passion!). You will probably also eat a variety of grains, which have health benefits. Gluten-free eating also tends to be richer in whole foods because processed foods so often contain gluten. When you cook your food at home, you tend to use healthier ingredients than what is used in restaurants, and this can have positive effects on your cholesterol levels and digestive health.

Children can have an especially hard time getting used to a new way of eating, particularly when they are old enough to be used to typical kid fare. Look at the gluten-free lifestyle as an opportunity to introduce them to a new, healthier way of life. Try to make it fun and let them choose new fruits and vegetables to try. Ask them to take part in the cooking process and teach them how to make some of their favorite foods in a gluten-free version. If they are part of the process, they might actually find it fun!

The Key to a Balanced Breakfast

A healthy breakfast contains a balance of complex carbohydrates and protein. With the variety of recipes in this book, you will have no problem coming up with nutritious, balanced breakfast ideas every day. You will even find some creative ways to incorporate vegetables into your breakfast routine. Eating a balanced breakfast can help you with weight loss and overall health and wellness. Try incorporating a new smoothie into your breakfast routine each week. Save leftover vegetables from dinner and add them to eggs for a nutritious start to your day. Think outside the box and get creative! Breakfast doesn't have to be sweet.

Cooking Equipment You'll Need

Gluten-free cooking isn't much different from regular cooking when it comes to kitchen equipment. A well-stocked kitchen will include a mixer, an electric blender, a food processor, and an assortment of pots and pans. A slow cooker is useful to have, and there is an entire chapter in this book dedicated to slow cooker recipes. A waffle maker is necessary if you plan to make waffles, and an electric skillet can be extremely helpful when making pancakes and French toast. You will also want a frying pan small enough to make omelets and crepes. While it is not necessary, it is fun to have a set of doughnut pans, and there are a few recipes for baked doughnuts in this book.

Once you have your kitchen stocked with the necessary food supplies and equipment, you're ready to give gluten-free cooking a try! Don't be discouraged if your first attempts don't turn out as good as you hope. With some trial and error, you will soon be making delicious gluten-free foods with the best of them!

CHAPTER 2

Eggs and Omelets

Fried Eggs Over Easy

A fried egg is incredibly versatile and the basis for many meals. This method of cooking will produce a fried egg with cooked whites and runny yolks. If you like your whites a bit runny, don't cook them quite as long on the first side. If you like your yolks hard, cook them for an additional 30–60 seconds on the second side.

INGREDIENTS | SERVES 1

2 extra-large eggs
1 tablespoon butter
⅛ teaspoon salt, or to taste
⅛ teaspoon ground black pepper, or to taste

The Incredible Edible Egg!

Eggs are nutritious, affordable, and naturally gluten-free. In fact, eggs are a rich source of vitamin A, B vitamins, calcium, choline, phosphorus, lecithin, and iron. Latest science shows that the cholesterol found in eggs does not significantly impact blood cholesterol levels, and most health and medical professionals agree that one egg a day is good for you. If you can find them, local farm fresh eggs with their rich, bright orange yolks are the best!

1. Crack 2 eggs into a coffee cup. Set aside. (You don't want to crack the eggs directly in the pan in case you accidently get a piece of shell in there. If you do get a bit of shell in the cup, use an egg shell to retrieve it.)

2. Heat a small cast-iron skillet or nonstick frying pan over medium-low heat and add the butter to the pan. (You will need at least 1 tablespoon to keep the eggs from sticking to the pan.)

3. When the butter is sizzling but not yet turning brown, gently pour the eggs into the pan. Season with salt and pepper. Let the eggs cook slowly over medium-low heat for 2–3 minutes, or until the whites have just started to look opaque, but aren't yet hard.

4. Gently turn the eggs with a spatula, one at a time, being careful not to break the yolks. Reduce heat to low and cook for another 20–30 seconds, then slide them onto a plate.

Perfect Poached Eggs

Poached eggs are wonderful on toast (gluten-free, of course!) or served over asparagus or a tomato. They are also the basis for the popular Eggs Benedict. Poaching an egg is a great way to enjoy this nutrient-dense food without the added fat you get when you fry or scramble them.

INGREDIENTS | SERVES 1

2 teaspoons apple cider vinegar (optional; omit if sensitive to vinegar)

1 teaspoon salt

1 extra-large egg

⅛ teaspoon ground black pepper (optional)

Tips for the Perfect Poached Eggs

Adding vinegar to the water you use to cook your eggs is not essential, but it does help the egg hold together. Fresh eggs are easier to poach and hold together better, so use the freshest eggs you can find, especially when you're new to this cooking technique. You can poach up to two eggs together in a 2-quart saucepan. To poach a larger batch, use a large sauté pan and do not swirl the water.

1. Place a 2-quart saucepan filled with 2" of water over medium heat. Add the vinegar (if using) and salt and bring to a simmer (you do not want the water to boil).

2. Meanwhile, break an egg into a coffee cup. It is much easier to slide it into the pot from a cup.

3. When the water is simmering, use a spoon to stir it in one direction until the water is swirling around. Carefully drop the egg into the center of the "whirlpool." This helps keep the egg together in the water. You can use a spatula to help it along if you need to.

4. Turn off the heat, and cover the pan for exactly 5 minutes. Do not lift the lid, tempting though it may be. Have a slotted spoon ready to retrieve the egg when it's done. After 5 minutes, carefully lift the egg out with the slotted spoon and serve immediately with a sprinkle of pepper, if desired.

Shirred Eggs with Crumbled Cheddar Topping

These are just plain cute and so appealing. For an extra touch, you can place a thin slice of tomato in the bottom of each ramekin.

INGREDIENTS | SERVES 6

¼ cup butter
12 extra-large eggs
¼ teaspoon salt
¼ teaspoon ground black pepper
¾ cup grated Cheddar cheese

An Elegant Touch

If you are having a crowd of people to brunch, place ramekins on a cookie sheet and bake for 10 minutes. Then serve with a big bowl of fruit on the side. You can use glass custard cups, but individual ramekins made of white porcelain are more elegant.

1. Preheat oven to 350°F. Grease 12 small 4-ounce ramekins with butter; place the ramekins on a cookie sheet.

2. Break 1 egg into each of the prepared ramekins. Sprinkle the eggs with salt and pepper and dot with butter (about ⅓ tablespoon per egg).

3. Sprinkle with Cheddar and bake for 8–12 minutes. Serve immediately.

Spinach with Baked Eggs and Cheese

This makes a nutritious breakfast or a nice addition to any brunch.

INGREDIENTS | SERVES 4

1½ cups gluten-free corn bread crumbs (see Chapter 7 for Corn Bread recipe)
3 (10-ounce) packages frozen spinach, thawed, moisture squeezed out
2 tablespoons butter, melted
½ cup shredded Swiss cheese
½ teaspoon ground nutmeg
¼ teaspoon salt
¼ teaspoon ground black pepper
1 cup heavy cream
8 large eggs

1. Preheat oven to 325°F. Grease a 10" × 10" glass baking dish with butter and sprinkle with the corn bread crumbs.

2. Mix together the spinach, butter, cheese, nutmeg, salt, and pepper. Stir in the heavy cream. Spread the spinach-cheese mixture in the bottom of the prepared pan.

3. Using the back of a tablespoon, make 8 depressions in the spinach mixture. Nest the raw eggs in their holes. Bake for 20 minutes or until the eggs are firm but not hard.

Herbed Baked Eggs for One

Submitted by Trina O'Boyle, OBoyOrganic.com, this dish is easy for one, but good enough that you can make them for a crowd on a Sunday for brunch.

INGREDIENTS | SERVES 1

2 teaspoons butter, divided

1 slice gluten-free sandwich bread such as Udi's Gluten Free Bread

1 slice smoked Gouda, Swiss, fontina, or Gruyère cheese

¼ teaspoon minced garlic

1 teaspoon minced fresh dill

1 teaspoon freshly grated Parmesan cheese

2 large eggs

1 teaspoon heavy cream

¼ teaspoon salt

¼ teaspoon ground black pepper

1. Preheat the broiler to high for 5 minutes and place the oven rack 6" below the heat source.

2. Spread 1 teaspoon butter on the bread and place it under the broiler until toasted on one side. Once toasted, remove and add the slice of cheese. Place under the broiler again until melted. Remove from the broiler; set aside.

3. In a small bowl, combine the garlic, dill, and Parmesan; set aside.

4. Carefully crack 2 eggs into a bowl; set aside.

5. Place a medium ovenproof dish on a medium baking sheet. Place the cream and remaining 1 teaspoon butter in the dish; place under the broiler for about 1–2 minutes, until hot and bubbly. Quickly but carefully, pour the eggs into the dish and sprinkle evenly with the herb mixture, salt, and pepper. Place back under the broiler for 3–5 minutes, until the whites of the eggs are almost cooked. (Rotate the baking sheet once if they aren't cooking evenly.)

6. The eggs will continue to cook after you take them out of the oven. Allow to set for 60 seconds before placing on the cheese bread.

Ricotta Torte with Serrano Ham and Parmesan

*If you can't find Serrano ham, substitute prosciutto. Do not, however,
use low-fat ricotta—it just doesn't taste the same.*

INGREDIENTS | SERVES 6

2 shallots, peeled and minced

2 tablespoons butter

3 large eggs

1 pound gluten-free ricotta cheese such as Organic Valley

½ cup grated Parmesan cheese

¼ cup finely chopped Serrano ham or prosciutto

1 teaspoon dried oregano

1 teaspoon dried basil

⅛ teaspoon ground nutmeg

½ teaspoon salt

½ teaspoon ground black pepper

1. Preheat oven to 325°F. In a medium skillet over medium heat, sauté the shallots in the butter for 2–3 minutes. Place the shallots in a pie pan that has been greased with butter.

2. In a large bowl, add the eggs and the rest of the ingredients; beat until well mixed and frothy. Pour into the prepared pie pan and bake for 35 minutes or until set and golden brown. Cut into wedges and serve.

Ricotta and Gluten

Because some brands use vinegar to curdle the ricotta and vinegar can sometimes contain gluten, it is important to make sure to buy ricotta cheese that is labeled gluten-free. If you're not sure, you can contact the manufacturer.

Shirred Eggs and Asparagus au Gratin

This is a very easy brunch or supper dish. Fresh asparagus is definitely better in this recipe than frozen. The trick is arranging the asparagus evenly in the pan.

INGREDIENTS | SERVES 4

1 pound fresh asparagus, ends trimmed
8 large eggs
½ cup freshly shredded Parmesan cheese
½ teaspoon salt
½ teaspoon ground black pepper

1. Preheat oven to 350°F.

2. Blanch the asparagus in boiling water for 5 minutes. Take out of the boiling water immediately and place in ice water and drain.

3. Prepare a medium casserole pan or dish with nonstick spray and arrange the asparagus in the bottom in a single layer. Break the eggs over the top of the asparagus. Sprinkle with the Parmesan, salt, and pepper, and bake until the eggs are done and the cheese is hot and runny (about 12 minutes). Serve hot.

Stir-Fry Brussels Sprout Scramble

Submitted by Heather McCurdy of www.realthekitchenandbeyond.com, this quick and easy egg scramble incorporates Brussels sprouts to make a nutritious breakfast.

INGREDIENTS | SERVES 2

½ pound Brussels sprouts, thinly sliced
1 tablespoon butter
4 large eggs, beaten
¼ teaspoon salt
⅛ teaspoon ground black pepper

In a medium sauté pan, sauté the Brussels sprouts in the butter over medium heat until soft and slightly golden brown on the edges, about 10 minutes. Add the eggs, salt, and pepper. Cook, stirring constantly, until the eggs are done, about 5 minutes. Serve immediately.

Cheesy Egg Cups

Refrigerate any leftover egg cups and the next morning you can heat them up in the microwave for a quick breakfast.

INGREDIENTS | MAKES 12

10 large eggs
½ cup whole milk
1 teaspoon salt
½ teaspoon ground black pepper
1 cup shredded Cheddar cheese
1 clove garlic, finely minced
1 tablespoon finely minced sweet onion or scallion

1. Preheat oven to 375°F. Butter a 12-cup muffin tin.

2. In a large mixing bowl, whisk together the eggs, milk, salt, and pepper.

3. In the bottom of the muffin cups, layer the cheese, then the garlic and onions or scallions, and then the egg mixture to fill each muffin cup about ¾ full. If you want, you can stir them up a bit with a fork to incorporate the eggs with the other ingredients.

4. Bake for about 25–30 minutes or until set. Remove from the oven and cool. They puff up like popovers and then deflate after they come out of the oven. Cool in the pan for about 5 minutes and then remove to a plate or wire rack. Serve warm or cool completely and refrigerate for later. Reheat in the microwave for a quick breakfast.

Broccoli and Cheese Egg Cups

This variation on the Cheesy Egg Cups (see this chapter) is a great way to get nutritious veggies onto your breakfast plate. This is also a fantastic way to use leftover vegetables from dinner. You can substitute spinach or asparagus for the broccoli.

INGREDIENTS | MAKES 12

10 large eggs

½ cup whole milk

1 teaspoon Lawry's Seasoned Salt or house seasoning

½ cup chopped steamed or roasted broccoli florets

½ cup shredded Cheddar cheese

1 tablespoon finely minced sweet onion or scallion

1. Preheat oven to 375°F. Butter a 12-cup muffin tin.

2. In a large mixing bowl, whisk together the eggs, milk, and Lawry's Seasoned Salt.

3. In the bottom of the muffin cups, layer the broccoli, the cheese, and the minced onion. Then add the egg mixture to fill each muffin cup about ¾ full. If you want, you can stir them up a bit with a fork to incorporate the cheese and veggies into the egg mixture.

4. Bake for about 25–30 minutes or until set. Remove from the oven and cool. Serve warm or cool completely and refrigerate for later. Reheat in the microwave for a quick breakfast.

Chicks in a Nest

These cute little breakfast cups have a hash brown crust and are filled with scrambled eggs. Serve with a side of bacon or sausage.

INGREDIENTS | MAKES 12

10 ounces shredded hash browns

7 large eggs

2 tablespoons gluten-free all-purpose flour such as Bob's Red Mill

2 tablespoons grated sweet onion

½ cup finely chopped precooked ham

½ cup shredded Cheddar cheese

2 tablespoons butter

¼ cup whole milk

½ teaspoon salt

¼ teaspoon ground black pepper

Chives for garnish

1. Preheat oven to 400°F. Grease a 12-cup muffin tin.

2. In a large mixing bowl, mix together the hash browns, 1 egg, the flour, onion, ham, and cheese. Press mixture into the muffin tins and bake for 30 minutes.

3. Meanwhile, melt 2 tablespoons butter in a medium skillet over medium-low heat. Whisk the 6 remaining eggs together with the milk, salt, and pepper. Add the egg mixture to the pan; cook over medium-low heat, stirring often, until the eggs are cooked through, about 3–5 minutes.

4. Spoon the scrambled eggs into the cooked hash brown cups. Garnish with chives.

Tex-Mex Egg White Scramble

Submitted by Karla Walsh, HealthfulBitesBlog.com. The mix of spices adds a nice Mexican touch in this quick and easy breakfast recipe, and the vegetables fill out the dish while keeping it surprisingly low in calories and high in fiber.

INGREDIENTS | SERVES 2

¾ cup diced butternut squash
⅓ cup diced green bell pepper
⅓ cup diced red onion
5 cherry tomatoes, quartered
¼ teaspoon chili powder
¼ teaspoon garlic powder
¼ teaspoon ground cumin
¼ teaspoon paprika
¼ teaspoon sea salt
¼ teaspoon ground black pepper, or to taste
6 egg whites (or 3 whole eggs if you prefer to include the yolks)

1. Heat a medium nonstick skillet over medium heat.

2. Place the butternut squash cubes in the pan and cook until lightly browned, 5–10 minutes. Add the bell pepper, onion, and tomatoes. Add the spices and stir to evenly coat all the vegetables. Cook until the vegetables begin to brown and soften, about 10 minutes, stirring occasionally.

3. Pour in the egg whites and cook until scrambled and firm, stirring so that the mixture is evenly cooked (about 5 minutes).

4. Spoon onto a plate and enjoy with a warmed corn tortilla.

Eggs Benedict with Asparagus

This classic breakfast dish is perfect for a special occasion. The recipe for Classic Hollandaise Sauce is in Chapter 11.

INGREDIENTS | SERVES 2

¼ cup Classic Hollandaise Sauce (see recipe in Chapter 11)
2 large eggs, poached
2 slices Canadian bacon
1 gluten-free English muffin, split
1 tablespoon soft butter
8 thin spears of asparagus, steamed

1. Make Classic Hollandaise Sauce according to directions in Chapter 11. Cover and keep warm while poaching the eggs (see recipe for Perfect Poached Eggs in this chapter for poaching directions).

2. While the eggs are poaching, heat a small skillet over medium heat and brown the Canadian bacon on both sides, about 2 minutes per side.

3. Toast the English muffins and spread with butter.

4. Assemble the Eggs Benedict by layering a slice of Canadian bacon on each English muffin half, top with asparagus spears, then a poached egg, and finally a drizzle of Hollandaise sauce.

Bacon and Veggie Egg Muffins

These tasty egg "muffins" can be made ahead for a quick warm-up in the morning.
These are basically mini quiches, and you will find a few variations in this chapter. Enjoy!

INGREDIENTS | MAKES 12

4 slices bacon, diced
½ medium sweet onion, small diced
½ green or red bell pepper, small diced
6 large eggs, beaten
1 cup whole milk
½ cup shredded Cheddar cheese
½ teaspoon salt
⅛ teaspoon ground black pepper
1 clove garlic, minced

1. Preheat oven to 350°F. Butter a 12-cup muffin tin.

2. In a medium skillet over medium heat, sauté the diced bacon until browned and crisp, about 8 minutes. Remove to a paper towel to drain. Add the diced onion and diced bell pepper to the bacon grease in the pan and sauté until soft and starting to brown, about 5 minutes.

3. Meanwhile, in a large liquid measuring cup, whisk together the eggs, milk, cheese, salt, and pepper.

4. Add the garlic to the peppers and onions, and continue to cook for 1 minute. Remove the vegetable from the heat.

5. Spoon the vegetable mixture evenly into the 12 muffin cups. Sprinkle the bacon evenly on top of the vegetables. Then pour the egg mixture evenly into each muffin cup, so that each cup is almost full.

6. Bake for about 20 minutes or until set. Remove from the oven and cool. Serve warm or cool completely and refrigerate for later.

Spinach and Feta Omelet

This vegetarian omelet is chock-full of iron, calcium, folate, and vitamins A, C, and K.

INGREDIENTS | SERVES 1

3 large eggs
¼ teaspoon salt, divided
2 tablespoons olive oil, divided
½ red onion, sliced thin
1 cup chopped baby spinach leaves
½ ounce feta cheese, crumbled

1. Whisk the eggs and ⅛ teaspoon of salt in a small bowl; set aside.

2. Heat an omelet pan over medium-low heat; add 1 tablespoon of olive oil, the sliced onions, and the remaining ⅛ teaspoon salt. Cook slowly, stirring occasionally for 3–5 minutes until the onions are soft and translucent. Add the remaining olive oil and the spinach leaves; cook for another 2–3 minutes or until the spinach is wilted.

3. Turn the heat down to low. Pour the eggs into the pan and swirl to coat. Cover the pan and allow the eggs to cook with the vegetables for 3–4 minutes or until they are solid and almost cooked through. Carefully slip the spatula underneath the omelet, tip the skillet to loosen it, and gently flip it over.

4. Sprinkle the eggs with the feta and cover for 2 minutes or until the cheese melts. Fold the omelet in half and serve immediately.

Western Omelet

A traditional Western Omelet contains ham, green pepper, and onion. This recipe also includes Cheddar cheese, but feel free to omit. You can also try it with Swiss cheese for a different flavor.

INGREDIENTS | SERVES 1

3 large eggs
¼ teaspoon salt, divided
2 tablespoons butter, divided
¼ cup diced sweet onion
¼ cup diced green bell pepper
¼ cup diced cooked ham
¼ cup shredded Cheddar cheese
Tabasco sauce (optional)

1. Whisk the eggs and ⅛ teaspoon salt in a small bowl; set aside.

2. Melt 1 tablespoon butter over medium heat in an omelet pan. Add the onions, green pepper, and the remaining ⅛ teaspoon salt and cook until translucent, stirring occasionally. Add the ham and cook for another minute.

3. Add the remaining butter and allow it to melt. Add the beaten egg to the pan and swirl the pan so it coats evenly. Turn the heat down to low and cover the pan. Allow the eggs to cook for 3–4 minutes or until they are solid and almost cooked through. Carefully slip the spatula underneath the omelet, tip the skillet to loosen, and gently flip it over.

4. Sprinkle with the cheese and cover for 2 more minutes while the cheese melts. Fold the omelet in half and serve immediately with a sprinkle of Tabasco sauce, if desired.

Bacon, Mushroom, and Tomato Omelet

The bacon adds a salty crunch to this colorful omelet.

INGREDIENTS | SERVES 1

3 large eggs
¼ teaspoon salt, divided
2 slices bacon
2 tablespoons butter, divided
¼ cup sliced button mushrooms
1 clove garlic, finely minced
¼ teaspoon dried oregano
⅛ teaspoon ground black pepper
¼ cup diced tomato
¼ cup shredded fontina cheese

1. Whisk the eggs with ⅛ teaspoon salt in a small bowl; set aside.

2. In a medium skillet over medium heat, cook the bacon for 2–3 minutes per side. Crumble or chop into small pieces; set aside.

3. Place 1 tablespoon of butter in an omelet pan over medium heat and add the mushrooms, garlic, oregano, and ⅛ teaspoon salt and pepper. Cook for about 5 minutes, stirring occasionally, until the liquid is evaporated.

4. Add the remaining tablespoon of butter and allow it to melt. Sprinkle the bacon and tomatoes over the mushrooms and add the beaten egg to the pan. Turn the heat down to low and cover, allowing the eggs to cook for 3–4 minutes or until they are solid and almost cooked through. Carefully slip the spatula underneath the omelet, tip the skillet to loosen, and gently flip it over.

5. Sprinkle with the cheese and cover for 2 more minutes while the cheese melts. Fold the omelet in half and serve immediately.

Chard and Parmesan Omelet

*Like beets, chard is a unique source of phytonutrients called betalains,
which provide antioxidant, anti-inflammatory, and detoxification support.
This omelet is perfect for springtime with Swiss chard fresh from the garden.*

INGREDIENTS | SERVES 1

3 large eggs
¼ cup whole milk
¼ teaspoon salt, divided
2 tablespoons olive oil, divided
½ small red onion, sliced thin
1 cup sliced Swiss chard leaves
½ ounce Parmesan cheese,
coarsely grated
⅛ teaspoon ground black pepper

1. Whisk the eggs, milk, and ⅛ teaspoon salt in a small bowl; set aside.

2. Heat an omelet pan over medium-low heat, and add 1 tablespoon of olive oil, the sliced onions, and ⅛ teaspoon salt. Cook slowly, stirring occasionally for 3–5 minutes until the onions are soft and translucent. Add the remaining olive oil and the Swiss chard and cook for another 3–5 minutes or until the chard is wilted.

3. Turn the heat down to low. Pour the eggs into the pan and swirl to coat. Cover the pan and allow the eggs to cook with the vegetables for 3–4 minutes or until they are solid and almost cooked through. Carefully slip the spatula underneath the omelet, tip the skillet to loosen it, and gently flip it over.

4. Sprinkle the eggs with the Parmesan cheese and the pepper. Fold the omelet in half and serve immediately.

Crab Omelet with Hollandaise Sauce

This elegant omelet is perfect for company.

1. Whisk the eggs, milk, ⅛ teaspoon salt, and pepper in a small bowl; set aside.

2. Heat 1 tablespoon of butter in an omelet pan over medium-low heat. Add the eggs and cook slowly for 3–5 minutes, using a spatula to lift up the sides to allow the raw egg to run underneath, until almost set.

3. Meanwhile, mix the crabmeat with the shallot and 1 tablespoon of the scallions in a small bowl. When the eggs are almost set, spoon most of the crabmeat mixture (reserve a tablespoon or two for garnish) in a line down the center of the eggs in the pan. Add goat cheese on top of the crabmeat.

4. Carefully slip the spatula underneath the omelet, tip the skillet to loosen it, and gently fold it in half. Slide it onto a serving plate and spoon Classic Hollandaise Sauce over the top. Garnish with the remaining crabmeat and scallions.

Chorizo and Potato Omelet

If you have leftover potatoes from dinner the night before, this omelet comes together quickly. Otherwise you can parboil the potatoes while the chorizo is cooking and then add them to the pan with the onions.

INGREDIENTS | SERVES 1

1 link chorizo sausage
½ small red onion, sliced thin
½ cup cooked potatoes, cubed
3 large eggs
⅛ teaspoon salt
⅛ teaspoon ground black pepper
1 ounce Cheddar cheese, shredded
1 tablespoon salsa (optional)

1. Heat a 7" omelet pan over medium heat. Remove the chorizo from its casing and add to the pan. Cook until it's cooked through, browned, and crumbly, about 10 minutes; transfer to a paper towel to drain.

2. Add the sliced onion and potato to the remaining sausage grease in the hot pan. Cook over medium heat, stirring occasionally until they start to brown, about 10 minutes.

3. Meanwhile, whisk the eggs with the salt and pepper in a small bowl. Return the chorizo to the pan and pour the beaten eggs evenly over the sausage and veggies.

4. Reduce heat to low and cook slowly until the eggs are set, about 5 minutes. You can lift up the sides with the spatula to allow the raw egg to run underneath.

5. When the eggs are almost set, sprinkle half the omelet with the cheese and gently fold it in half. Cook for another minute and then slide it onto a serving plate and top with salsa if desired.

Salmon Omelet

This omelet is full of omega-3 fatty acids. It is well-seasoned and will surely become a breakfast staple.

INGREDIENTS | SERVES 2

3 tablespoons olive oil, divided
¼ cup chopped green onions
1 cup trimmed and chopped asparagus
1 tablespoon chopped fresh dill
1 (6-ounce) salmon steak
6 large eggs, beaten

1. In a large skillet over medium heat, combine 1 tablespoon olive oil, green onions, asparagus, and fresh dill. Sauté until the asparagus is soft, 7–10 minutes. Transfer to a bowl and set aside.

2. In the same skillet, add another tablespoon olive oil and sauté the salmon over medium heat until flaky, about 10 minutes depending on the thickness of the steak. Transfer to the bowl with the asparagus and use a fork to gently break up the salmon and toss with the asparagus; set aside.

3. Wipe out the skillet and add the remaining tablespoon of olive oil. Add the beaten eggs to the pan and cook until lightly browned, about 5 minutes per side.

4. Place the salmon and asparagus mixture on half of the egg, fold over, and serve.

Paleo Breakfast Bowl

This breakfast is a bit more exciting than the ordinary breakfast you might be used to. Nitrate-free, uncured bacon is a real treat.

INGREDIENTS | SERVES 1

2 tablespoons olive oil
½ cup diced uncured bacon
1 cup diced asparagus
2 large eggs

1. Heat the olive oil in a small skillet over medium-high heat.

2. Cook the bacon and asparagus in the skillet until the asparagus is not quite tender, about 8–10 minutes. Remove to small bowl.

3. In the same skillet, cook the eggs over easy (do not flip) for about 5 minutes. Be sure that yolks are runny.

4. Place the cooked eggs on top of the bacon mixture in the bowl.

5. Mix and serve.

Cremini and Broccoli Omelet with Fontina

The buttery, nutty flavor of the fontina is the perfect complement to the broccoli and cremini mushrooms in this omelet.

INGREDIENTS | SERVES 1

3 tablespoons butter, divided
2 tablespoons sliced scallions
4 medium broccoli florets, chopped
4 cremini mushrooms, sliced
3 large eggs
2 tablespoons whole milk
⅛ teaspoon salt
⅛ teaspoon ground black pepper
¼ cup shredded fontina cheese

1. Heat 2 tablespoons butter in a frying pan over medium-low heat. Sauté the scallions and broccoli for 4–5 minutes, until they're starting to brown. Add the mushrooms and sauté for another 2–3 minutes or until they're soft. Set aside.

2. Heat the remaining butter in a 7" omelet pan over medium-low heat. Whisk the eggs, milk, salt, and pepper in a bowl and pour into the pan. Cook slowly until the eggs are set, about 5 minutes. Lift up the sides with the spatula to allow the raw egg to run underneath.

3. When the eggs are almost set, sprinkle half the omelet with the cheese and vegetables. Gently fold in half, cook another minute, and slide onto a serving plate.

Cheddar, Bacon, and Bell Pepper Omelet

For a sweet and salty combination, try this combination of bell pepper, bacon, and Cheddar.

INGREDIENTS | SERVES 1

3 large eggs
¼ teaspoon salt, divided
2 tablespoons butter, divided
1 tablespoon diced sweet onion
1 tablespoon diced green bell pepper
2 tablespoons shredded Cheddar cheese
¼ teaspoon ground black pepper
2 strips cooked bacon, crumbled

1. Whisk the eggs and ⅛ teaspoon salt in a small bowl; set aside.

2. Melt 1 tablespoon butter over medium heat in an omelet pan. Add the onions, green pepper, and ⅛ teaspoon salt and cook until the onions are translucent, stirring occasionally, about 5–7 minutes.

3. Add the remaining butter and allow it to melt. Add the beaten egg to the pan and swirl the pan so it coats evenly. Turn the heat down to low and cover the pan. Allow the eggs to cook for 3–4 minutes or until they are solid and almost cooked through.

4. Carefully slip the spatula underneath the omelet, tip the skillet to loosen, and gently flip it over.

5. Sprinkle with the cheese and pepper and cover for 2 more minutes while the cheese melts. Sprinkle half the omelet with bacon, fold it in half, and serve immediately.

CHAPTER 3

Quiche and Frittatas

Ham Quiche with Caramelized Onions, Swiss Chard, and Broccoli

The secret to this delicious quiche is to cook the onions slowly over low heat until they are caramelized and sweet.

INGREDIENTS | SERVES 4

2 red onions, peeled and sliced thin

5 tablespoons butter, divided

5 large eggs

1 cup whole milk

1 teaspoon salt

½ teaspoon ground black pepper

1 cup rinsed and finely chopped broccoli florets

1 cup Swiss chard leaves (rinsed and torn into bite-size pieces)

1 cup shredded Cheddar cheese

4 ounces ham, diced

1. Preheat oven to 350°F.

2. In a medium skillet, cook the onions in 2 tablespoons butter over low heat, stirring occasionally, for 25–30 minutes or until they are soft, light brown, and caramelized.

3. Meanwhile, butter a quiche pan or 9" pie plate with 1 tablespoon butter. In a large mixing bowl, whisk together the eggs, milk, salt, and pepper. Set aside.

4. Remove the caramelized onions from the pan and set aside.

5. Add 2 tablespoons butter to the pan; raise the heat to medium-low and sauté the broccoli florets for 4–5 minutes. Add the Swiss chard and sauté for 2–3 more minutes.

6. Spread the shredded cheese in the bottom of the quiche dish and layer the greens and onions on top. Add a layer of diced ham and pour the egg and milk mixture evenly over the filling.

7. Bake for 30–35 minutes, until the top is golden brown and the eggs are set in the middle. Allow it to stand for 10–20 minutes before serving.

8. Serve warm or at room temperature with a side salad for a complete meal.

Italian Peppers and Spinach Quiche

This recipe was submitted by Lauryn Blakesley, TheVintageMom.com.
Not only is this quiche gluten-free, but it is vegetarian as well!

INGREDIENTS | SERVES 4

1 (9") gluten-free pie crust (optional)

2 tablespoons extra-virgin olive oil

1 medium sweet onion, chopped

3 cloves fresh garlic, sliced thin

1 (16-ounce) jar Rose Romano's Italian Peppers Marinara with Red Bell Pepper, or your favorite chunky Italian marinara, divided (you will only need ¾ of the jar)

2½ cups fresh baby spinach (torn into small pieces)

¾ cup grated smoked Gouda cheese

¾ cup shredded mozzarella cheese

4 large eggs

¾ cup whole milk

½ cup fresh-grated Parmesan cheese

With or Without

This recipe can be made with or without the pie shell. If you use a prepared gluten-free pie crust, cook it until browned before adding the ingredients.

1. Preheat oven to 350°F. If using, bake the pie crust according to package directions.

2. Meanwhile, in a medium skillet over medium-low heat, heat the extra-virgin olive oil and sauté the onions and garlic until the onions are translucent, about 10 minutes.

3. Add ½ jar of the marinara and cook, stirring constantly until simmering.

4. Add the spinach and cook until it's wilted, about 1 minute.

5. Add the marinara mixture to the pie plate; top with the Gouda and mozzarella.

6. In a large bowl, whisk together the eggs, milk, and ¼ jar of marinara sauce; pour over the cheese and spinach mixture. Top with grated Parmesan.

7. Bake for 40 minutes or until the top is golden brown and the eggs are set in the middle. Allow it to stand for 10–20 minutes before serving.

Bacon, Spinach, and Gruyère Quiche

The Gruyère cheese gives this quiche a richness that is impossible to resist.

INGREDIENTS | SERVES 6

8 ounces bacon

1 small sweet onion, sliced thin

10-ounce box frozen spinach, thawed and drained

6 large eggs

2 cups whole milk

1½ cups shredded Gruyère cheese

½ cup fresh-grated Parmesan cheese

2 teaspoons chopped fresh thyme

½ teaspoon salt

¼ teaspoon ground black pepper

1. Cook the bacon in a large skillet over medium heat until it's crispy (about 2–3 minutes per side). Transfer it to paper towels to cool.

2. Add the onion to the remaining bacon fat in the pan and cook over low heat until soft and translucent, 10–15 minutes.

3. Meanwhile, squeeze the water out of the spinach. When the onions are soft, add the spinach to the pan and continue cooking for 1–2 more minutes, until wilted. Remove from the heat and allow it to cool.

4. In a large bowl, whisk together the eggs and milk. Add the cheeses, thyme, salt, and pepper.

5. Crumble the bacon into a buttered 9" deep-dish pie plate. Spread the spinach and onions on top of the bacon and then pour the egg mixture over the top.

6. Bake for 45–50 minutes or until the top is golden brown and the eggs are set in the middle. Allow it to stand for 10–20 minutes before serving.

Mushroom, Chard, and Ham Quiche

Chard is best in the spring or fall when it's fresh and young.
You can substitute spinach if you can't find chard.

INGREDIENTS | SERVES 6

1 tablespoon butter
½ cup sliced cremini mushrooms
1 bunch Swiss chard
8 large eggs
1 cup whole milk
½ teaspoon salt
½ teaspoon ground black pepper
2 ounces ham, chopped
1 cup shredded baby Swiss cheese

Mushroom 101

The cremini mushroom, also referred to as "baby bella," is a young version of the meaty portobello mushroom. Cremini mushrooms generally have a firmer texture and more flavor than white button mushrooms, which, incidentally, are just a younger version of the cremini. You can certainly use white button mushrooms in this recipe, but the creminis give it a richer taste.

1. Preheat oven to 350°F and grease a 9" deep-dish pie plate.

2. Melt the butter in a large skillet over medium-low heat. Add the mushrooms and sauté for 3–4 minutes or until they start to soften. Add the chard, cover, and cook until wilted, about 5 minutes, stirring once or twice. Remove from the heat and let cool.

3. In a large bowl, whisk together the eggs, milk, salt, and pepper. Spread the ham in the bottom of the pie plate. Layer the mushrooms and chard on top, then the cheese, and pour the egg mixture over the top.

4. Cook for 45–50 minutes or until the eggs are set and it's lightly browned on top. Remove from the oven and let it sit for 5–10 minutes before serving.

Italian Sausage Quiche

The heavy cream makes this quiche decadent and delicious!

INGREDIENTS | SERVES 6

1 pound sweet Italian sausage
½ small onion, chopped
¼ cup chopped red bell pepper
4 ounces Cheddar cheese, shredded
4 large eggs
1 cup heavy cream
1 teaspoon minced fresh parsley
1 teaspoon minced fresh basil
¼ teaspoon ground black pepper
⅛ teaspoon salt
⅛ teaspoon garlic powder

1. Preheat oven to 375°F.

2. In a large skillet over medium heat, cook the sausage, onion, and red pepper until the sausage is browned, about 10–12 minutes. Drain and spread the mixture in a 9" pie plate or a square casserole dish. Sprinkle the shredded cheese over the sausage.

3. In a large bowl, whisk the eggs, cream, and herbs/ seasonings together and pour over the top of the sausage.

4. Bake for 35–40 minutes or until cooked through. (Test by inserting a knife in the middle. If it comes out clean, then it is done). Let stand for 10–15 minutes before cutting. Serve warm or at room temperature.

Roasted Beet, Tomato, and Spinach Mini Quiches

Submitted by Lauryn Blakesley, TheVintageMom.com.
These colorful mini quiches are packed with nutrients.

INGREDIENTS | YIELDS 6

6 large eggs

1 cup whole milk

1½ cups shredded Dubliner cheese
(or Cheddar)

½ cup roasted beets

1 cup chopped spinach

¾ cup chopped tomato

¼ cup chopped sweet onion

1. Preheat oven to 375°F and grease a muffin tin.

2. Whisk the eggs and milk together in a large bowl. Add the cheese and chopped vegetables. Stir to combine.

3. Pour into the prepared muffin tin and bake for 18–20 minutes or until the middle bounces back and is not runny.

How to Roast Beets

Wash and peel the beets. Toss them with enough olive oil to coat and ¼ teaspoon salt and ¼ teaspoon pepper. Spread in a single layer on a large baking pan and roast in a 425°F oven for 25 minutes or until soft. Store in an airtight container in the refrigerator. Roasted beets are a wonderful addition to salads and, of course, quiche!

Ham and Jarlsberg Cheese Mini Quiches

Mini quiches are perfect for taking to a potluck or brunch. They are easy to serve and there's no mess.

INGREDIENTS | YIELDS 12

1 package gluten-free pie crust mix
(such as Glutino)
2 large eggs
½ cup grated Jarlsberg cheese
¼ cup minced prosciutto or smoked ham
⅔ cup heavy cream
⅛ teaspoon grated nutmeg
2 tablespoons minced fresh chives
½ teaspoon ground black pepper

1. Preheat oven to 325°F. Grease a 12-cup mini muffin pan with nonstick spray and prepare the pie crust mix according to box directions. Roll out thinly.

2. With a 2" biscuit cutter (or using the rice-floured rim of a juice glass), cut the dough into 12 rounds and line the muffin cups with dough.

3. Pulse the remaining ingredients in a food processor to combine.

4. Fill the cups ¾ full with the cheese mixture.

5. Bake for about 10 minutes, or until the quiches are set. Let rest for 5 minutes. Carefully lift the mini quiches from the cups. Serve warm.

Potato-Crusted Dairy-Free Spinach Quiche

Submitted by Kelly Dabel, WholesomeDinnerTonight.blogspot.com, this quiche is a warm and satisfying dish and hearty enough to stand alone as your main entrée. If you prefer not to go dairy-free, you can use whole milk and top the quiche with your favorite cheese after it is done baking.

INGREDIENTS | YIELDS 4

2 medium russet potatoes, peeled
1 tablespoon olive oil, divided
3 ounces Canadian bacon, diced
1 clove garlic, finely minced
2 tablespoons diced red onion
1 cup cooked spinach
4 eggs, well beaten
¾ cup rice milk

1. Preheat oven to 425°F.

2. Using a mandoline, thinly slice the peeled potatoes.

3. Drizzle ½ tablespoon oil in the bottom of a 9" glass pie plate; layer potato slices over the bottom and sides of the pie plate, slightly overlapping each slice.

4. Bake the potatoes for 25 minutes.

5. Meanwhile, in a large sauté pan add ½ tablespoon oil and the diced Canadian bacon; sauté over medium heat for 5–10 minutes or until golden brown and fragrant.

6. Add the garlic and onion and sauté until tender, about 10 minutes; add cooked the spinach and cook until warmed through, about 1–2 minutes. Remove the bacon/spinach mixture from the heat and allow to cool slightly.

7. In a large bowl, mix together the eggs, milk, and cooled spinach mixture (if it's too hot it will scramble your eggs).

8. Remove the potato crust from the oven and decrease oven temperature to 375°F. Pour the egg and spinach mixture over the potatoes, smoothing evenly with a spatula. Bake for 30–40 minutes or until the eggs are set. Remove from the oven and let it sit for 5–10 minutes before serving. (Top with cheese if you like.)

Seaweed Quiche

Submitted by Sherry Aikens, SuperExhausted.com. Seaweed has a sea smell when it is eaten plain, but once placed in other foods, you will never know it is in there. Mixing it with spinach is a great way to introduce seaweed into your diet. You can't taste the seaweed, but it packs a nutritional punch.

INGREDIENTS | SERVES 6

1 tablespoon butter

1 medium onion, diced small

1 pound boneless, skinless chicken breasts, diced

¼ teaspoon salt

¼ teaspoon ground black pepper

1 (10-ounce) box frozen chopped spinach, thawed and water pressed out

8 large eggs

2 cups whole milk

2 tablespoons hot sauce

2 cups shredded sharp Cheddar cheese

½ cup dried nori roasted seaweed

½ cup gluten-free bread crumbs (optional)

Health Benefits of Seaweed

Seaweed contains high amounts of calcium and almost as much protein as legumes. It's also a great source of vitamins B_{12} and A and soluble fiber. You can find it in Asian markets, some grocery stores, and Trader Joe's.

1. Preheat oven to 375°F. Add the butter to a large frying pan and sauté the onions over medium heat until lightly brown and translucent, about 10 minutes. Add the diced chicken and season with salt and pepper; cook until the chicken is browned and cooked through, about 10 minutes. Remove to a bowl and set aside.

2. Place the spinach in the frying pan and cook over low heat to remove any excess moisture.

3. Add the spinach to the bowl with the onion and chicken; add the eggs, milk, hot sauce, cheese, and seaweed. Stir to combine.

4. Grease a 9" × 13" pan and sprinkle bread crumbs over the bottom (optional). Pour the egg mixture into the pan. Cook for 40–45 minutes or until the eggs are set in the middle. Let it set for 10–15 minutes before serving.

Kale Frittata with Genoa Salami

Frittatas make an easy, nutritious breakfast and this is a great way to use up all that kale you get from the summer CSA. The genoa salami adds warmth to this dish.

INGREDIENTS | SERVES 4

3 tablespoons butter
1 medium red onion, sliced
1 bunch fresh kale, leaves only
½ cup diced genoa salami
8 large eggs
½ cup shredded mozzarella cheese
1 teaspoon salt, divided
¼ teaspoon ground black pepper
½ cup grated Parmesan cheese

1. Preheat oven to 375°F.

2. Heat the butter in a large ovenproof skillet over medium-low heat; add the onion and sauté until tender and translucent, about 5 minutes.

3. Add the kale to the skillet and sprinkle with ½ teaspoon salt; stir gently until the kale begins to wilt and the liquid evaporates, about 2–3 minutes.

4. Raise the heat to medium and add the genoa salami. Cook until heated through, about 2 minutes.

5. Meanwhile, in a medium mixing bowl whisk together the eggs, mozzarella cheese, remaining ½ teaspoon salt, and the pepper; add to the kale/salami mixture.

6. Sprinkle the Parmesan cheese on top and transfer the skillet to the oven for 10–15 minutes or until the cheese on top is a light golden brown and the eggs are cooked through. Serve warm or at room temperature.

Potato Frittata with Cheese and Herbs

This recipe is highly versatile, so experiment with different herbs and cheeses.

INGREDIENTS | SERVES 4

1 large Yukon gold potato, peeled
2 tablespoons butter
¼ teaspoon salt
¼ teaspoon ground black pepper
6 large eggs
½ cup grated Parmesan cheese
6 sage leaves, minced
Fresh herbs of choice, extra cheese, and sour cream to garnish

Striking Yukon Gold

Yukon gold potatoes were developed in the 1970s at the University of Guelph, Ontario, Canada. They were initially slow to capture the market, but now are widely popular. They are particularly suited for baking, salads, and soup.

1. Using a mandoline, slice the potato as thinly as possible. Melt the butter in a heavy 12" frying pan.

2. Add the potatoes, making a thin layer, and season with salt and pepper. Cook over medium heat for 10 minutes (this will be the crust).

3. In a medium bowl, beat the eggs well. Add the cheese and minced sage. Pour over the potatoes and turn down the heat to the lowest possible setting. Cook for 10 minutes.

4. When the eggs have set, place the frittata under the broiler until golden brown on top, about 2–3 minutes. Cut into wedges and serve immediately with garnishes.

Asparagus Frittata

Some matches are made in heaven, and asparagus with eggs and cheese is a divine combination.

INGREDIENTS | SERVES 4

1 (10-ounce) box frozen chopped asparagus
3 tablespoons butter
6 large eggs
1 cup grated Cheddar cheese
¼ cup shredded Monterey jack or pepper jack cheese
1 teaspoon lemon zest
¼ teaspoon salt
¼ teaspoon ground black pepper

1. Cook the asparagus according to package directions and drain.

2. Melt the butter in a heavy 12" skillet over medium-high heat.

3. In a medium bowl, beat the eggs; mix in the cheeses, lemon zest, and salt and pepper.

4. Pour the egg-cheese mixture into the pan, evenly distribute the asparagus, and reduce heat to low, cooking very slowly for 10–15 minutes.

5. Place under preheated broiler for 10 seconds or until nicely browned.

Sausage Broccoli Frittata

Broccoli is high in vitamins C and A and folate (and also soluble fiber), so dig in!

INGREDIENTS | SERVES 6

1 tablespoon olive oil

½ pound breakfast sausage, crumbled

1 cup chopped broccoli, steamed or roasted

1 cup diced cooked potato

¼ teaspoon salt

¼ teaspoon ground black pepper

8 large eggs

½ cup grated Parmesan cheese

1. Preheat oven to 375°F. Heat olive oil in a large, oven-safe frying pan over medium heat. Add the sausage and cook until no longer pink, 10–15 minutes.

2. Add the cooked broccoli and potato. Stir until heated through, about 2 minutes. Add the salt and pepper.

3. In a medium bowl, whisk the eggs. Add the eggs to the skillet and cook for another 1–2 minutes. Sprinkle with cheese and transfer to the oven.

4. Bake for 10–15 minutes or until the eggs are set. Broil for an additional 2–3 minutes until nicely browned on top. Serve warm or at room temperature.

Veggie Cheese Frittata

*Submitted by Renee Mayk. For a vegan version, try this recipe
with coconut milk and Daiya Cheddar shreds.*

INGREDIENTS | SERVES 2

2 tablespoons olive oil or butter

½ cup chopped orange, red, or green bell peppers

⅓ cup chopped red onion

⅓ cup chopped tomato

½ cup thinly sliced zucchini or chopped asparagus

1 tablespoon chopped basil

⅛ teaspoon salt

⅛ teaspoon ground black pepper

2 large eggs

¼ cup whole milk

½ cup cottage cheese

¾ cup shredded Cheddar cheese

¼ cup shredded Monterey jack cheese

1 tablespoon chopped parsley

1. Heat the olive oil in an medium ovenproof skillet over medium heat.

2. Place the peppers, onions, tomatoes, and zucchini in the skillet and sauté until they start to soften, 5–10 minutes. Add the basil, salt, and pepper and continue to cook for 3–4 minutes or until the veggies are just beginning to brown.

3. Meanwhile, with a handheld blender, thoroughly combine the eggs, milk, cottage cheese, and Cheddar cheese. Turn on the broiler.

4. Pour the egg mixture over the vegetables in the skillet. Cover and cook on medium-low heat for 3 minutes or until the vegetable portion is set and the top is still mostly wet.

5. Transfer the skillet to the oven under the broiler and cook about 4 minutes until the top portion is set. Sprinkle with Monterey jack cheese and broil for another 1 or 2 minutes until melted. Garnish with parsley and serve warm.

Potato, Ham, and Spinach Frittata

Spinach is a great source of calcium, so eat up! This hearty frittata will stick with you all day long.

INGREDIENTS | SERVES 6

2 tablespoons olive oil

1 large potato, sliced thin

1 small Vidalia onion, halved and sliced thin

¼ teaspoon salt, divided

8 large eggs

1 (10-ounce) box frozen chopped spinach, thawed and squeezed dry

⅛ teaspoon ground black pepper

1 ounce deli ham, cut into small squares

1 cup shredded Cheddar or Parmesan cheese

1. Preheat oven to 375°F. Heat the olive oil in a large cast-iron skillet over medium heat. Place the sliced potatoes and onions in the pan, sprinkle with ⅛ teaspoon salt, and reduce heat to medium-low. Sauté until soft and beginning to brown, about 15 minutes.

2. Meanwhile, whisk the eggs in a large bowl until light and fluffy. Add the remaining salt and the pepper. Stir in the spinach, ham, and cheese.

3. Pour the egg mixture into the pan with the potatoes and onions. Bake for 15 minutes or until the eggs are set. Serve hot or at room temperature.

Use Up Your Leftovers

Frittata is a staple in Italy—putting a lot of eggs together with leftover or fresh vegetables is a fine way of using every precious bit of food. Frittata can be jazzed up with herbs, cheeses, and hot red pepper flakes or it can be child-mild for young kids. The only thing to remember about frittatas is that just about anything goes!

Savory Shrimp Quiche

Submitted by Astacia Carter, Mamikaze.com. Shrimp make this quiche a gourmet delight.

INGREDIENTS | SERVES 12

6 slices Swiss cheese

2 prepared gluten-free pie crusts

1 medium yellow onion, diced

1 pound (41–50 count) raw shrimp, peeled and roughly chopped

2 cloves garlic, minced

6 large leaves fresh basil, chopped

2 stems fresh oregano leaves, plucked and chopped

1 cup spinach leaves

12 large eggs

¼ cup heavy cream

½ teaspoon salt

½ teaspoon ground black pepper

½ tablespoon red pepper flakes, or to taste

1. Preheat oven to 375°F. Place Swiss cheese in the bottom of the pie crusts; set aside.

2. Sauté the onion in a skillet over medium heat for 5–8 minutes, until translucent. Add the chopped shrimp, garlic, and herbs. Cook with the lid on for about 3 minutes. Add the spinach, replace the lid, and remove from heat.

3. In a large bowl, combine the eggs, cream, salt, pepper, and red pepper flakes; whisk for 2 minutes. Fold in the shrimp mixture. Carefully pour into the prepared pie plates.

4. Cover with aluminum foil and bake for 30 minutes or until firm. Test with knife. Let cool for 5 minutes before cutting.

CHAPTER 4

Breakfast Sandwiches and Wraps

Smoked Sausage and Hash Brown Breakfast Wrap

Submitted by Heather, RealtheKitchenandBeyond.com. Packed with smoked sausage, hash browns, eggs, and Cheddar, these breakfast wraps deliver the perfect diner breakfast to go!

INGREDIENTS | SERVES 4

1 tablespoon olive oil

1 large potato, peeled and shredded

½ small Vidalia onion, diced

1 smoked sausage link, thinly sliced and quartered

¼ teaspoon salt

⅛ teaspoon ground black pepper

6 large eggs

2 ounces Cheddar cheese, shredded

4 gluten-free tortillas, any flavor (such as Rudi's)

1. Heat the oil in a medium frying pan over medium heat. Add the potato, onion, sausage, salt, and pepper. Cook, stirring often, until the potatoes and onions are soft, about 5–8 minutes.

2. In a medium bowl, beat the eggs until frothy. Add the eggs to the potato mixture, stirring constantly until well cooked, about 5–8 minutes.

3. Remove from the heat and add the Cheddar. Divide the mixture evenly among the wraps and serve immediately.

Fried Egg and Cheese Sandwich

This traditional breakfast sandwich is just as delicious on gluten-free bread.

INGREDIENTS | SERVES 1

2 slices gluten-free bread, such as Udi's Gluten Free Bread

1 tablespoon butter

2 large eggs

⅛ teaspoon salt

⅛ teaspoon ground black pepper

1 thin slice Colby jack or Cheddar cheese

1. Toast the bread.

2. Meanwhile, heat the butter in a medium frying pan over medium heat. Fry the eggs, about 2–3 minutes per side. Season with salt and pepper.

3. Assemble the sandwiches by placing the eggs on a slice of toast. Top with cheese and then the remaining slice of toast. Cut in half and serve immediately.

Grilled Bacon and Cheese Sandwich

*This variation on a classic grilled cheese sandwich is perfect for breakfast.
You can even throw a fried egg on it, if you desire.*

INGREDIENTS | SERVES 1

2 tablespoons butter, softened and divided

2 slices gluten-free bread such as Udi's Gluten Free Bread

4 ounces Provolone cheese, thinly sliced

2 slices cooked bacon

1. Spread ½ tablespoon butter on one side of each slice of bread. Assemble the sandwich by layering the cheese and bacon in between the slices of bread, butter side out.

2. Heat a frying pan over medium-low heat and add the remaining tablespoon of butter to the skillet to melt. Place the sandwich in the pan and toast until golden brown, about 3 minutes per side. Flip and finish toasting until golden brown. Remove from pan, slice, and serve.

Egg and Avocado Wraps

This nutritious breakfast is loaded with healthy fats, folate, and vitamin E.

INGREDIENTS | SERVES 4

4 gluten-free wraps, such as Rudi's Gluten Free Tortillas

1 tablespoon mayonnaise, divided

4 slices cooked ham

4 large eggs, scrambled

1 avocado, sliced

1. Lay a wrap on a plate and spread with ¼ tablespoon mayonnaise. Place a slice of ham on top.

2. Spoon the eggs on top of the ham in a line down the middle. Place a few slices of avocado on top of the eggs. Roll up and serve.

Sausage Egg Sandwich

Just because you're gluten-free doesn't mean you can't enjoy one of America's most iconic breakfast sandwiches at home.

INGREDIENTS | SERVES 6

1 pound breakfast sausage

6 large eggs

6 gluten-free English muffins, such as Glutino Gluten Free English Muffins

6 teaspoons butter, softened

6 slices American cheese

Gluten-Free Wraps

Many brands now make gluten-free tortillas and wraps. It takes some trial and error to find ones that are soft and foldable. Rudi's is an excellent choice. Also Julian Paleo wraps can be purchased online.

1. Form six sausage patties and fry them in a large frying pan over medium heat until they are cooked through and browned on the outside, about 10 minutes. Use a spatula to flatten them so they will fit nicely onto a sandwich.

2. Remove the sausage from the pan and drain on paper towels. Fry the eggs in the remaining sausage grease, about 3 minutes per side. If you prefer the scrambled version, you can break them up in the pan while they're cooking, making sure to keep each one separate.

3. Meanwhile, split the English muffins and toast them. Spread the insides with butter, about 1 teaspoon per side or to taste.

4. When the eggs are almost done, flip them and lay a slice of cheese on top of each. Cook for another 30 seconds before removing from the pan.

5. Assemble sandwich by layering the bottom of an English muffin with a sausage patty, an egg topped with cheese, and finally the top of the English muffin. Repeat to make the remaining sandwiches. Serve immediately.

Canadian Bacon, Egg, and Cheese Muffin

Canadian bacon is the perfect shape to fit on an English muffin, but feel free to make this recipe with regular bacon slices if you desire.

INGREDIENTS | SERVES 2

2 slices Canadian bacon

1 tablespoon butter

2 large eggs, beaten

2 gluten-free English muffins, split

1 tablespoon mayonnaise

2 slices Cheddar cheese

1. In a small frying pan over medium heat, cook the Canadian bacon until lightly browned on each side, 4–5 minutes. Remove from the pan.

2. Add the butter to the pan and fry the eggs for about 3 minutes per side. If you prefer the scrambled version, you can break them up in the pan while they're cooking, making sure to keep them separate.

3. Meanwhile, split the English muffins and toast them. Spread the insides with ½ tablespoon mayonnaise each.

4. When the eggs are almost done, flip them and lay a slice of cheese on top of each. Cook for another 30 seconds before removing from the pan.

5. Assemble sandwich by layering the bottom of an English muffin with a slice of bacon, an egg topped with cheese, and finally the top of the English muffin. Repeat with the second sandwich. Serve immediately.

Sausage Gravy over Corn Bread Doughnuts

Sausage gravy is a traditional Southern dish, generally served over biscuits.
For a twist, try this over the Corn Bread Doughnuts in Chapter 6.

INGREDIENTS | SERVES 4

1 pound breakfast sausage

⅓ cup gluten-free all-purpose flour

4 cups whole milk

½ teaspoon salt

1 teaspoon ground black pepper

4 Corn Bread Doughnuts (see recipe in Chapter 6), or gluten-free biscuits

Sausage Gravy

Sausage gravy is a traditional Southern breakfast dish. If you haven't tried it, you don't know what you're missing! And there's no need to deprive yourself just because you're gluten-free. This recipe uses gluten-free, all-purpose flour to make the roux, and you can serve it over your favorite gluten-free biscuit or for a switch, over the Corn Bread Doughnuts in Chapter 6.

1. In a large frying pan over medium heat, crumble the sausage and brown until cooked through and no longer pink, about 10 minutes.

2. Reduce heat to low and sprinkle with flour. Stir the flour into the sausage. Add the milk, stirring constantly. Continue to cook, stirring frequently, for 10–15 minutes or until thickened to desired consistency. Season with salt and pepper. Add additional milk if too thin if desired.

3. Meanwhile, split the Corn Bread Doughnuts in half. Toast them lightly to warm them up if they're not fresh from the oven.

4. Spoon sausage gravy over the warm Corn Bread Doughnuts and serve immediately.

Egg, Bacon, and Gruyère with Aioli and Arugula

The aioli and arugula brings this ordinary breakfast sandwich up a notch or three, making it a gourmet dish worthy of company.

INGREDIENTS | SERVES 1

2 slices gluten-free bread

1 slice Gruyère cheese

1 teaspoon Simple Aioli (see sidebar), or mayonnaise

½ tablespoon butter

1 large egg

¼ teaspoon salt

¼ teaspoon ground black pepper

2 slices bacon, cooked

½ cup fresh arugula, washed and drained

Simple Aioli

For a gourmet treat, try making homemade aioli. Just place 2 cloves of garlic, 1 teaspoon Dijon mustard, and 1 large egg in the bowl of a food processor and process until combined. Then, keeping the motor running, slowly add 1 cup olive oil in a thin stream until completely combined. Finally, add 2 teaspoons lemon juice and a sprinkle of salt and process until thoroughly mixed. It will keep for up to 3 days in the refrigerator.

1. Preheat oven broiler to high. Place the bread on a sheet pan. Broil until golden brown on top, about 2 minutes; watch carefully so they don't burn. Remove from the oven and flip the slices over. Place the Gruyère on top of one bread slice. Return the pan to the oven and broil until the plain bread slice is golden brown and the cheese is melted on the other slice, about 2 minutes. Remove and spread the plain bread slice with aioli.

2. Meanwhile, heat the butter in a large frying pan over medium heat. Fry the egg, about 3 minutes per side. Sprinkle with salt and pepper.

3. Assemble the sandwich by layering the bacon slices on the cheese-topped bread slice. Then place the eggs on top. Add a handful of arugula on top of the egg and cover with the remaining bread slice. Cut in half and serve immediately.

Egg, Prosciutto, and Pesto Muffins

The crispy prosciutto and savory pesto make these egg sandwiches extra special.

INGREDIENTS | SERVES 2

1 ounce thinly sliced prosciutto
1 tablespoon butter
2 large eggs
¼ teaspoon salt
¼ teaspoon ground black pepper
2 gluten-free English muffins
4 teaspoons prepared pesto

1. In a small frying pan over medium heat, cook the prosciutto until lightly browned on each side, a minute or two per side. Remove from the pan.

2. Add the butter to the pan and fry the eggs for about 3 minutes per side; season with salt and pepper.

3. Meanwhile, split the English muffins and toast them. Spread each of the insides with 1 teaspoon pesto. Divide the prosciutto evenly among the English muffin bottoms. Place the eggs on the prosciutto and top with the remaining muffin halves.

Egg Salad Sandwich with Bacon and Avocado

Egg salad isn't just for lunch! Top it with bacon and avocado for a nutritious breakfast sandwich.

INGREDIENTS | SERVES 2

3 large hard-boiled eggs
3 tablespoons mayonnaise
¼ teaspoon yellow mustard
¼ teaspoon salt
¼ teaspoon ground black pepper
2 gluten-free English muffins, split
2 slices cooked bacon
½ avocado, sliced

1. Peel and mash the hard-boiled eggs. Add the mayonnaise and mustard and sprinkle with salt and pepper; stir to combine.

2. Toast the English muffins. Divide the egg salad, bacon, and avocado between the muffins to form the sandwiches.

Strawberry, Banana, and Nutella Sandwich

Who says breakfast sandwiches have to be savory? This decadent breakfast sandwich combines chocolate hazelnut spread with strawberries and bananas for a fresh and delicious morning treat.

INGREDIENTS | SERVES 2

4 slices gluten-free bread

2 tablespoons butter, softened

4 tablespoons Nutella

2 strawberries, sliced

½ banana, sliced

1. Toast the bread and spread each slice with the butter and Nutella.

2. Layer the sliced strawberries and bananas over the Nutella on 2 bread slices, then top each with the remaining slices. Serve immediately.

Southwestern Breakfast Taco

These quick and easy breakfast burritos have a delightful Southwestern flair. Add salsa or guacamole for even more flavor.

INGREDIENTS | SERVES 2

1 tablespoon butter

½ cup diced red or green bell pepper

¼ cup diced red onion

4 large eggs, lightly beaten

¼ teaspoon salt

⅛ teaspoon ground black pepper

2 slices bacon, cooked crisp and crumbled

2 (8") gluten-free wraps, such as Rudi's Gluten Free Tortillas

4 slices Cheddar cheese

1 tablespoon chopped parsley

¼ cup salsa

1. Melt the butter in a large nonstick skillet over medium heat. Add the bell pepper and onion and sauté for 5 minutes.

2. Stir the eggs, salt, and pepper into the vegetables in the skillet; cook just until the eggs are soft, about 3–4 minutes. Remove from heat; stir in the bacon.

3. Warm the wraps according to package directions. Immediately layer the cheese over the wraps; top with salsa and the egg mixture and fold wraps over filling.

Croque Madame

This French version of a ham and cheese sandwich is topped with an egg,
making it equally at home on the breakfast table as it is at lunch.

INGREDIENTS | SERVES 2

4 slices gluten-free sandwich bread

2 teaspoons Dijon mustard, divided

½ cup shredded Gruyère cheese

6 ounces thinly sliced gluten-free deli ham

1 tablespoon butter

1 cup Basic Cream Sauce (see recipe in Chapter 11)

2 large eggs, fried sunny-side up or over easy

Beware of Hidden Gluten in Deli Meats

Deli meats are often sources of hidden gluten, so be sure to purchase brands that expressly state on the packaging they are gluten-free. If you have celiac disease or are highly sensitive to traces of gluten, let the personnel at the deli counter know of your allergy so they can avoid cross-contamination. Many deli counters offer special allergen-free equipment, or they should be willing to clean off one of the machines for you. It's also best to request that they open a new package of meat or cheese in case the open ones have been contaminated by the shared machines.

1. Lay the bread slices on a large rimmed baking sheet. Spread each with ½ teaspoon of Dijon mustard. Distribute the Gruyère and ham evenly between two of the bread slices. Top with the remaining slices, mustard side down.

2. Melt the butter in a large frying pan over medium heat. Cook the sandwiches on both sides until golden brown and the cheese is melted, 2–3 minutes per side. Return the sandwiches to the baking pan and pour the cream sauce over the top. Broil in the oven for 2 minutes or until the sauce is bubbly.

3. Remove from the oven, top each sandwich with a fried egg, and serve immediately.

Breakfast Empanada Muffins

Adapted from Noelle Kelly's Breakfast Empanada Muffins at SingersKitchen.com, this Mexican-inspired breakfast sandwich is made with prepared gluten-free English muffins to make it quick and easy. Don't skip the Manchego cheese. That's what makes these really pop!

INGREDIENTS | SERVES 4

5 large eggs

2 tablespoons water

½ teaspoon salt

½ teaspoon ground black pepper

2 tablespoons olive oil

½ red onion, sliced thin

½ poblano pepper (red or green), seeded and diced

½ cup button mushrooms, chopped

½ cup drained cooked black beans

¼ teaspoon dried oregano

1 cup shredded Manchego cheese (divided)

4 gluten-free English muffins, such as Glutino Gluten Free English Muffins

Prepared salsa

1. Preheat oven to 350°F. In a medium bowl, crack the eggs and whisk to combine. Add the water, salt, and pepper and set aside.

2. Heat the oil in a large frying pan over medium heat. Sauté the onions, peppers, and mushrooms for 7 minutes on medium heat and then add the egg mixture and cook for 5–7 minutes.

3. Add the black beans and oregano and cook for another 5 minutes. Add ½ cup cheese and mix.

4. Split the English muffins and lay them on a baking sheet. Place 2 tablespoons egg mixture on each muffin half and top with more cheese.

5. Bake for 20–22 minutes. Let cool for 5 minutes and serve with salsa.

Manchego Cheese

Manchego is a delicious hard cheese made of sheep's milk from the La Mancha region of Spain. The buttery, nutty flavor is lovely in egg dishes or enjoyed alone with a glass of Spanish wine.

Peanut Butter, Banana, and Honey Sandwich

This is a fabulous post-workout breakfast. It's the perfect combination of natural sugars, protein, and healthy fats.

INGREDIENTS | SERVES 1

1 slice gluten-free sandwich bread
½ tablespoon butter
1 tablespoon natural peanut butter
½ banana, sliced thin
1 tablespoon raw honey

Toast the bread until lightly browned. Spread with the butter and then the peanut butter. Lay the bananas on top in a single or double layer. Drizzle with honey and enjoy immediately.

Tex-Mex Eggs on Corn Bread Doughnuts

The Corn Bread Doughnuts (see recipe in Chapter 6) lend a crisply corn flavor to this hearty breakfast sandwich.

INGREDIENTS | SERVES 2

2 Corn Bread Doughnuts (see Chapter 6)
2 slices Monterey jack cheese
2 large eggs, fried
Salsa for dipping

1. Using a serrated knife, cut the Corn Bread Doughnuts in half. Heat under a broiler, cut sides up, until lightly browned, about 2 minutes.

2. Lay a slice of Monterey jack cheese on each of the doughnut bottoms. Place a fried egg on top of each and cap each sandwich with the remaining doughnut tops. Serve with salsa for dipping.

CHAPTER 5

Breakfast Casseroles and Skillets

Cheese Strata

This overnight breakfast casserole is perfect for holiday brunches or other festive morning occasions.

INGREDIENTS | SERVES 8

⅓ cup butter

½ teaspoon dry mustard

1 clove fresh garlic, minced

10 slices gluten-free white bread, crusts removed

2 cups shredded sharp Cheddar cheese

2 tablespoons chopped fresh parsley

2 tablespoons chopped yellow onion

½ teaspoon salt

½ teaspoon Worcestershire sauce

⅛ teaspoon ground black pepper

4 large eggs

2½ cups whole milk

Make-Ahead Casseroles for Easy Mornings

A make-ahead casserole is the perfect dish to serve guests because it can be made the night before. This allows you to focus on your guests rather than being tied to the kitchen. Just be sure to allow plenty of time to bring the casserole to room temperature before baking.

1. In a small bowl, mix together the butter, dry mustard, and garlic. Spread on the bread slices. Cut the bread slices into thirds.

2. Line the bottom and sides of an ungreased 8" × 8" baking dish with buttered bread thirds, buttered sides down.

3. In a large bowl, mix together the Cheddar cheese, parsley, onion, salt, Worcestershire, and pepper. Spread evenly over the bread. Top with the remaining bread slices, buttered sides up.

4. In a bowl, beat the eggs and stir in the milk, and then pour over the bread. Cover and refrigerate overnight.

5. The next morning, heat the oven to 325°F. Bake the strata uncovered for 1 hour and 15 minutes or until puffed and golden brown on top. Let cool for 10–15 minutes before cutting. (The casserole will fall in the middle.)

Potato and Sausage Breakfast Casserole

Submitted by Kelly Moeggenborg, KellytheKitchenKop.com. This nutritious casserole is a great dish to serve for brunch, and you can freeze individual servings to warm up quickly in the toaster oven on busy school mornings.

INGREDIENTS | SERVES 12

7 cups shredded potatoes

1 teaspoon salt

1 large yellow onion, shredded

⅓ cup butter, melted

12 large eggs, beaten

3 cups whole milk

¼ teaspoon ground black pepper

2 pounds sausage, fried and crumbled

4 cups shredded Cheddar cheese

1. Preheat oven to 425°F and grease a 14" × 11" glass baking dish with butter.

2. In a large bowl, mix together the potatoes, salt, onion, and melted butter and press into the bottom of the glass dish. Bake for 30 minutes. Remove from oven and reduce heat to 350°F.

3. Meanwhile, combine the eggs, milk, and pepper in a medium mixing bowl.

4. When the potato crust is baked, sprinkle with the fried sausage and shredded Cheddar cheese. Pour the egg/milk mixture over the top and bake for 30 minutes or until set. Let cool and cut into squares.

Hash Brown Breakfast Casserole

Submitted by Mary Carver, GivingUponPerfect.com. This hearty breakfast casserole will stick with you all day.

INGREDIENTS | SERVES 12

8 large eggs

1 cup whole milk

¼ teaspoon salt, or to taste

¼ teaspoon ground black pepper, or to taste

1½ pounds shredded hash browns

¾ pound breakfast sausage, browned

2 cups shredded Cheddar cheese

1. Preheat oven to 350°F. Grease a 9" × 13" pan.

2. Whisk the eggs and milk together and add the salt and pepper.

3. Sprinkle the hash browns in the bottom of the pan. Sprinkle the browned sausage over the hash browns. Pour the egg mixture over the sausage and hash browns. Sprinkle cheese on top.

4. Bake for 45–50 minutes or until it doesn't run when you cut into it.

French Toast Casserole

Submitted by Melissa Jennings, StockpilingMoms.com. This is an easy way to make French toast for a crowd. No standing over the griddle, making each piece one by one. Gluten-free cinnamon raisin bread is recommended for this recipe, but you can use plain bread if you prefer.

INGREDIENTS | SERVES 6

1 loaf gluten-free cinnamon raisin bread (Udi's recommended)
6 large eggs
1 cup whole milk
1 teaspoon salt
1 teaspoon ground nutmeg
1 teaspoon ground cinnamon
⅔ cup vegetable oil
1 teaspoon vanilla extract
½ cup granulated sugar

1. Grease an 8" × 8" baking dish and place the bread in the dish, arranging it so it covers the bottom and is level.

2. In a large bowl, combine the eggs, milk, salt, nutmeg, cinnamon, oil, vanilla, and sugar. Pour the egg mixture over the bread. Cover and refrigerate overnight.

3. The next morning, heat the oven to 450°F and bring the casserole to room temperature. Bake for 25–30 minutes or until set. Serve with maple syrup.

Ham 'n' Cheese Egg Bake

Submitted by Arlene Metricarti. This is another casserole that you will want to prepare the night before you serve it, making it a wonderful dish for company.

INGREDIENTS | SERVES 12

1½ cups shredded Cheddar cheese
1½ cups shredded mozzarella cheese
2 tablespoons butter
½ pound fresh button mushrooms, sliced
6 green onions, sliced
1 medium red bell pepper, chopped
1¾ cups cubed fully cooked ham
12 large eggs
2 cups heavy cream
¼ teaspoon salt
¼ teaspoon ground black pepper

1. Sprinkle the cheeses into a greased 9" × 13" baking pan.

2. In a large skillet over medium heat, melt the butter and sauté the mushrooms, onions, and red pepper in butter until soft, 5–8 minutes. Stir in the ham to warm through. Spoon over the cheese.

3. In a separate bowl, combine the eggs, cream, salt, and pepper. Pour over the ham mixture. Cover and refrigerate overnight.

4. The next morning, heat oven to 350°F and set the casserole on the counter to come to room temperature. Bake uncovered for 35–45 minutes or until a knife inserted comes out clean. Let cool for 10–15 minutes before cutting.

Bacon and Potato Bake

Submitted by Melissa Angert, girlymama.com. This dish combines the quintessential breakfast flavors of bacon, eggs, cheese, and potatoes into a convenient make-ahead breakfast casserole.

INGREDIENTS | SERVES 12

¾ pound sliced bacon

1 bunch green onions, chopped (about ¼ cup)

4 cups diced hash brown potato cubes, thawed

1½ cups shredded pepper jack cheese

1½ cups shredded Cheddar cheese

4 large eggs

1 cup whole milk

½ teaspoon salt

¼ teaspoon ground black pepper

Green Onions vs. Scallions

Scallion is the group name for many members of the onion family. A green onion is a new onion harvested while its top is still green and its bulb is small. Although true scallions are a bit milder than green onions, the two can be used interchangeably in recipes.

1. Cook the bacon in a large frying pan over medium heat until browned and crispy, about 6–8 minutes. Remove to paper towels to drain.

2. Add the onions to the remaining bacon grease and cook for 2–3 minutes or until tender and fragrant.

3. Place the potatoes in a greased 9" × 13" baking dish. Sprinkle the cheeses evenly over the potatoes. Layer the onions and the crumbled bacon on top.

4. In a large bowl, whisk together the eggs, milk, salt, and pepper. Pour over the potato mixture in the pan. Cover and refrigerate overnight or for 7–8 hours.

5. The next morning, heat the oven to 350°F and bring the casserole to room temperature. Bake for 40–45 minutes or until the cheese is bubbly, but not brown. Allow to stand 15 minutes before cutting.

Gruyère-Swiss Cheese Strata with Spinach and Onions

Submitted by Trina O'Boyle, OboyOrganic.com. The Gruyère makes this dish a special treat. The mild yet distinctive flavor makes it perfect for a dinner party dish.

INGREDIENTS | SERVES 9

10 large eggs
4 cups whole milk
1 teaspoon dry mustard
1 packed cup fresh spinach
1 cup thinly sliced and diced red onion
¼ teaspoon salt
¼ teaspoon ground black pepper
5 cups cubed gluten-free bread
3 cups shredded Gruyère and Swiss cheese mix

For the Love of Gruyère

Gruyère cheese is sweet yet slightly salty. Its distinctive but not overpowering taste makes it a versatile baking cheese. It also melts beautifully, making it a popular choice for French onion soup and fondue. Try shredding some into your macaroni and cheese to kick the flavor up a notch!

1. In a large bowl, whisk together the eggs, milk, dry mustard, spinach, red onion, salt, and pepper. Set aside.

2. Spread the bread cubes in a greased 9" × 13" baking dish and sprinkle with the cheese.

3. Pour the egg mixture over the bread and cheese and cover for at least 4 hours, or overnight.

4. In the morning, preheat oven to 350°F and bake for at least 1 hour, until the strata is nice and fluffy and the egg is cooked in the middle.

Green Chili Egg Bake

Submitted by Jessie Weaver, JessieWeaver.net, this is an overnight egg casserole with a Southwestern twist: Delicious green chilies bring wonderful flavor to basic breakfast eggs and potatoes.

INGREDIENTS | SERVES 6

4 cups shredded hash browns, thawed

½ teaspoon garlic powder

½ teaspoon salt

8 ounces ham or Canadian bacon, diced

4 ounces chopped green chilies (canned)

1 cup shredded sharp Cheddar cheese

6 large eggs

1¼ cups whole milk

¼ cup sour cream

¼ teaspoon ground black pepper

1. Spread the hash browns in a greased 8" × 8" casserole dish and sprinkle with garlic powder and salt.

2. Layer the ham, green chilies, and cheese on top of the hash browns.

3. In a medium bowl, whisk together the eggs, milk, sour cream, and pepper. Pour evenly over the casserole. Cover and refrigerate overnight.

4. The next morning, heat the oven to 375°F and bring the casserole to room temperature. Bake for 1 hour or until eggs are set. Let cool for 10 minutes before cutting.

Berry Croissant Puff

The buttery croissants combined with cream cheese and berries make for a lightly sweet breakfast treat. Perfect for summer occasions when the fruit is fresh.

INGREDIENTS | SERVES 9

3 large gluten-free croissants (such as Schar)

1½ cups fresh or frozen raspberries and/or blueberries

8 ounces cream cheese, softened

½ cup granulated sugar

2 large eggs

1 cup whole milk

1 teaspoon vanilla extract

Sweetened whipped cream for topping

1. Preheat oven to 350°F. Cut the croissants into 1" pieces and spread them in the bottom of a greased 9" × 9" square baking pan. Sprinkle the berries on top.

2. In a mixing bowl, beat the cream cheese, sugar, and eggs until smooth and creamy. Slowly add the milk and then the vanilla, mixing the whole time. Pour over the croissants and allow it to set for 30–60 minutes.

3. Bake for 35–40 minutes or until it is set and golden brown on top. Serve warm with whipped cream on top.

French Toast Apple Bake

Submitted by Melissa Angert, girlymama.com. The apple pie filling makes it very easy to put this dish together. Better still, you can make it the night before to save time in the morning.

INGREDIENTS | SERVES 12

¾ cup butter, melted

1 packed cup light brown sugar

1 teaspoon ground cinnamon

2 (21-ounce) cans apple pie filling

8 large eggs

2 cups whole milk

1½ teaspoons pure vanilla extract

18 slices gluten-free white bread

1. Grease a 9" × 13" baking dish. Pour the melted butter into the dish and sprinkle with the brown sugar and cinnamon. Top with the apple pie filling.

2. In a medium mixing bowl, whisk together the eggs, milk, and vanilla. Layer the bread slices on top of the apple pie filling, pressing down firmly. Alternate layers of bread with the egg mixture so every layer is thoroughly saturated. Pour slowly to avoid spillovers.

3. Cover with aluminum foil and refrigerate overnight. Uncover and bake at 350°F for 1 hour. If desired, drizzle with syrup.

Sausage and Egg Casserole

This hearty casserole is traditionally made with day-old Italian bread, but you can use any gluten-free bread that you have and it will work just fine. It's a great way to use up bread that is drying out.

INGREDIENTS | SERVES 12

12 ounces breakfast sausage

½ cup diced yellow onion

6 large eggs

2 cups shredded sharp Cheddar cheese

2 cups whole milk

1 teaspoon salt

½ teaspoon dry mustard

¼ teaspoon ground black pepper

2 cups gluten-free bread cubes

1. Brown the sausage in a large frying pan over medium heat until cooked through, about 10 minutes. Add the onions and cook until translucent, about 5–8 minutes. Drain.

2. In a mixing bowl, whisk the eggs and stir in the cheese, milk, salt, dry mustard, and pepper. Add the bread cubes and stir to coat. Add the sausage and onions.

3. Transfer to a greased 9" × 13" baking pan. Cover and refrigerate overnight.

4. The next morning, heat oven to 350°F. Bring casserole to room temperature. Bake for 45–55 minutes or until the eggs are set. Let cool for 10 minutes before cutting.

Brunch Lasagna

This fun twist on lasagna is full of breakfast goodness. The ham and asparagus make it a lovely choice for a spring or Easter brunch.

INGREDIENTS | SERVES 12

½ cup butter

⅓ cup gluten-free all-purpose flour

½ teaspoon salt

¼ teaspoon ground black pepper

3 cups whole milk

1 teaspoon lemon juice

9 gluten-free lasagna noodles, cooked and drained (Tinkyada or DeBoles has a no-cook version that works well)

2 cups chopped ham

16 ounces frozen asparagus, defrosted, drained, and roughly chopped

2 cups shredded white Cheddar cheese

1 cup shredded Gruyère cheese

1. Preheat oven to 350°F. In a large saucepan, melt the butter over medium heat. Whisk in the flour, salt, and pepper. Add the milk and bring to a boil, stirring constantly. Cook and stir until thick, 3–4 minutes. Remove from the heat and stir in the lemon juice.

2. In a greased 9" × 13" baking pan, layer the following: ¼ cup of the prepared white sauce, 3 lasagna noodles, half the ham, half the asparagus, ⅓ cup Gruyère, and ¾ cup Cheddar. Repeat, starting again with ¼ cup white sauce. Top with the remaining noodles, white sauce, and cheeses.

3. Bake for 40–45 minutes or until bubbly around the edges and the cheese is lightly browned. Let it set for 15 minutes before cutting.

Broccoli Cheese Strata

Broccoli and Cheddar cheese is always a popular combination,
but add bacon and you have a delectable breakfast treat.

INGREDIENTS | SERVES 6

5 cups cubed day-old gluten-free bread, such as Udi's Gluten Free Bread

2 cups shredded Cheddar cheese

¼ cup finely chopped shallot

1 cup frozen broccoli florets, thawed and drained

1 cup chopped cooked bacon

10 large eggs

1½ cups whole milk

1. Butter a 9" × 13" baking dish and spread with half the bread cubes.

2. On top of the bread, layer the cheese, shallot, and half the broccoli and bacon. Top with the remaining bread.

3. In a large bowl, mix together 4 eggs and all the milk; pour evenly over the bread. Top with the remaining broccoli and bacon. Cover and refrigerate for 2 hours or overnight.

4. The next morning, heat the oven to 325°F and bring the strata to room temperature. Bake uncovered for 30 minutes.

5. After 30 minutes, remove from the oven, make 6 wells in the top of the strata, and pour an egg into each well. Bake an additional 20–25 minutes or until the eggs are set. Let stand for 15 minutes and serve.

Ham and Swiss Strata

This strata incorporates spinach for a nutritional punch. Try substituting Gruyère cheese for half the Swiss for extra flavor.

INGREDIENTS | SERVES 12

1 tablespoon butter
1 red bell pepper, diced
½ cup sliced scallions
1 (10-ounce) bag baby spinach
3 cups diced cooked ham
2 cups shredded Cheddar cheese
2 cups shredded Swiss cheese
5 cups cubed day-old gluten-free bread
8 large eggs
1½ cups whole milk
1 teaspoon dry mustard

1. In a large frying pan, melt the butter over medium heat and add the peppers and scallions. Sauté until they start to soften, about 5–8 minutes, and add the spinach. Cover and reduce heat to low for 2–3 minutes until wilted. Uncover and stir, mixing the spinach into the peppers and scallions. Remove from the heat.

2. In a buttered 9" × 13" baking dish, layer the ham, spinach mixture, half the cheeses, and the bread.

3. In a large bowl, whisk together the eggs, milk, and dry mustard. Pour evenly over the bread. Top with the remaining cheese. Cover and refrigerate for 4 hours or overnight.

4. The next morning, heat the oven to 325°F and bring the strata to room temperature. Bake covered for 30 minutes. Uncover and cook an additional 35–40 minutes or until the top is golden brown and the eggs are set. Let it set for 10–15 minutes before serving.

Persimmon and Sage Sausage Savory Bread Pudding

Submitted by Lindsay Cotter, CotterCrunch.com. This savory gluten-free bread pudding is loaded with calcium and is incredibly low in calories. The vanilla almond milk lends a bit of sweetness amidst the savory.

INGREDIENTS | SERVES 8

4 large eggs

¾ cup unsweetened vanilla almond milk (such as Silk Unsweetened Original Almond Milk)

2 tablespoons Dijon mustard

¼ teaspoon sea salt

¼ teaspoon freshly ground black pepper

¼ cup chopped fresh basil

¼ teaspoon minced garlic

4 large gluten-free bread slices cut into 1" cubes

2–3 cups fresh spinach

1 persimmon, diced (you can also use apple, tomato, or pear)

¾ cup diced cooked chicken sausage

1½ ounces Cheddar cheese, shredded

Chili pepper flakes for topping (optional)

1. Preheat oven to 400°F. Grease an 8" × 8" glass baking dish or casserole dish.

2. Whisk together the eggs and almond milk in a medium mixing bowl. Add the mustard, salt, pepper, chopped basil, and minced garlic; whisk to combine.

3. In a separate bowl, combine the bread, spinach, persimmon, and sausage. Add the egg and seasoning mixture and mix well, coating all the bread. Transfer to the prepared baking dish and press down to cover the bottom of the dish completely and evenly.

4. Bake for about 10–15 minutes, remove, and sprinkle the cheese on top. Bake for another 10 minutes, until the egg mixture looks almost fully cooked and the cheese is almost melted. Broil the last 3–4 minutes if desired in order to get the cheese browned and the corners crispy. Sprinkle with red pepper flakes if desired.

Sausage Potato Hash

This traditional breakfast skillet dish is naturally gluten-free. You can create many variations with different vegetables and types of potato and sausage.

INGREDIENTS | SERVES 6

2 tablespoons olive oil

3 medium Yukon gold or Idaho baking potatoes, diced

1 teaspoon Lawry's Seasoned Salt

1 small sweet onion, diced

½ green bell pepper, diced

1 pound ground sausage

1 cup shredded Cheddar cheese (optional)

6 large eggs

2 tablespoons butter

¼ teaspoon salt

¼ teaspoon ground black pepper

The Parboil

Potato hash is infinitely better if you parboil the potatoes before roasting them. You can skip this step and they will work out okay, but if you want the perfect crispy-on-the-outside, soft-on-the-inside texture, boil the diced potatoes in salted water for exactly 8 minutes. Drain immediately and shake them around in the colander or pan to rough up the edges. Then spread on the baking sheet and continue with the recipe as written.

1. Preheat oven to 400°F. Grease a large baking sheet with olive oil.

2. Spread the diced potatoes in a single layer on the prepared baking sheet, then drizzle with 1 tablespoon olive oil and sprinkle with Lawry's Seasoned Salt. Bake for 45–55 minutes or until they are nicely browned and crispy on the outside. Give the pan a shake about halfway through baking so they brown evenly.

3. Meanwhile, in a large skillet over medium-high heat, add the remaining 1 tablespoon oil and the diced onion and green pepper. Sauté for 2–3 minutes and then add the sausage. Sauté until cooked through and beginning to brown, about 10 minutes.

4. When the potatoes are done, remove them from the oven and carefully fold in the sausage mixture and the Cheddar cheese (if using). Set aside and keep warm.

5. In a clean medium skillet, fry the eggs in butter, about 2–3 minutes per side. Add the salt and pepper. Serve each plate with a serving of the sausage scramble and a fried egg on top.

Country Sweet Potato Breakfast Hash

Submitted by Jeremy Dabel, WholesomeDinnertonight.blogspot.com.
The sweet potatoes in this colorful dish give it a boost of nutrition,
perfect for sending the kids off to school in the mornings.

INGREDIENTS | SERVES 6

2 tablespoons extra-virgin olive oil, divided

3 strips of bacon, diced

1 shallot, finely chopped

1 sprig rosemary, finely chopped (leaves only)

1 small green or yellow zucchini, ¼" diced

1 pound small red potatoes, ¼" diced

2 large sweet potatoes, peeled and ¼" diced

¼ teaspoon paprika

¼ teaspoon chili powder

½ teaspoon garlic powder

¼ teaspoon sea salt

⅛ teaspoon ground black pepper

1. Heat a large skillet over medium-high heat and add 1 tablespoon oil and the bacon and shallots. Sauté for 2–3 minutes.

2. Add the rosemary leaves and zucchini and cook about 5 more minutes, until the zucchini is soft and cooked through.

3. Transfer the bacon-zucchini mixture to a plate. Add the potatoes and sweet potatoes along with the remaining oil to the pan. Add the spices, salt, and pepper. Reduce heat to medium-low and cook for about 10 minutes, stirring occasionally. If the potatoes are sticking and appear dry, add another tablespoon of oil.

4. Cook the potatoes until they are starting to brown, then add the bacon and zucchini to the pan and stir to combine. Serve hot.

Stuffed Breakfast Peppers

These stuffed peppers are nutritious and make a nice single-serve presentation at a brunch gathering.

INGREDIENTS | SERVES 8

2 pounds ground breakfast sausage

8 large bell peppers, any color

2 sweet onions, chopped

2 cloves garlic, minced

8 large eggs

¼ teaspoon salt

¼ teaspoon ground black pepper

1. Preheat oven to 350°F. Brown the sausage in a large skillet over medium heat, 5–8 minutes.

2. Meanwhile, cut the tops off the peppers and pull out the stems and seeds. Dice the pepper tops and add them to the skillet with the sausage, along with the chopped onion and minced garlic. Sauté until the onions are translucent, about 5 minutes.

3. Place the hollowed peppers in a 13" × 9" baking pan. Spoon the sausage mixture into the peppers, filling them about ¾ full. Cover with foil and bake for 30 minutes.

4. Remove the foil and make a small well in the middle of each pepper. Crack an egg into each one and return to the pan to the oven. Broil for 5–10 minutes, until the eggs are done to your liking. Sprinkle with salt and pepper and serve immediately.

Acorn Squash, Red Potato, and Andouille Sausage Hash

Submitted by Catherine Moss, EvolvingMotherhood.com, this colorful breakfast skillet looks like fall on a plate. The yolk works its way over the veggies and sausage giving everything a creamy richness.

INGREDIENTS | SERVES 4

2 tablespoons olive oil

2 tablespoons butter

½ small acorn squash, peeled and diced into ½" cubes (about 1½–2 cups)

2 medium red potatoes, diced into ½" cubes (about 1½–2 cups)

½ medium yellow onion, diced

2 cloves garlic, minced

¼ teaspoon smoked paprika

½ cup diced red bell pepper

½ cup diced green bell pepper

½ pound Andouille link sausage sliced

4 large eggs

¼ teaspoon salt

¼ teaspoon ground black pepper

Hot sauce, such as Frank's Red Hot or Sriracha (optional)

1. Using a large cast-iron skillet or sauté pan, heat the olive oil and butter over medium-high heat. Add the acorn squash, potato, onion, and garlic to the pan. Cook, stirring occasionally for about 10 minutes, or until the potato starts to soften.

2. Sprinkle the smoked paprika over the potatoes and squash and stir. Add the peppers and sausage to the pan. Stir occasionally to give all the sausage a chance to cook at the bottom of the pan. Cook for about 8 minutes or until the sausage is cooked through.

3. Using the back of a large spoon, make four indentations in the vegetable mixture. Crack an egg into each spot. Salt and pepper the eggs. Cover with a lid and cook for 3–5 minutes or until the egg whites are opaque white and cooked through and the yolks are still soft. Serve warm with a drizzle of hot sauce.

The Often Neglected Acorn Squash

Acorn squash, also called pepper squash, actually belongs to the same species as summer squashes such as zucchini, but it's popular in the fall and its shape resembles that of an acorn, thus the name. This squash is a good source of fiber and potassium and tastes good baked or stuffed with rice or meat mixtures.

Mexican-Style Breakfast Pizza

Submitted by Noelle Kelly, SingersKitchen.com, this Mexican-style breakfast pizza uses a masa base as the crust.

INGREDIENTS | SERVES 4

2 cups instant corn masa flour (Maseca Centroamericana recommended)

½ teaspoon salt, divided

1½ cups water

2 tablespoons olive oil, divided

4 large eggs

¼ teaspoon ground black pepper

¾ cup black beans, cooked and divided

¾ cup tomatillo salsa or green salsa, divided

1 cup shredded mozzarella or Monterey jack cheese, divided

½ teaspoon oregano, divided

Pickled jalapeño slices (optional)

Crema or sour cream (optional)

1. For the crust, combine the masa, ¼ teaspoon salt, and water and mix until well combined. It should not be dry; if it crumbles it requires more water. Add 1 tablespoon water at a time. Preheat oven to 400°F.

2. Divide the dough in half. Flatten one dough ball on a greased pizza pan until it is about 9" in diameter. Brush the crust with 1 tablespoon olive oil. Bake for 10 minutes. Remove from oven and repeat baking process with second crust.

3. Meanwhile, in a small bowl, whisk the 4 eggs until frothy. Add the remaining salt and the pepper. In a large frying pan, cook over medium heat until cooked and scrambled, about 2–4 minutes. Add the black beans to the eggs and mix well.

4. On each half-baked pizza crust, add half of the salsa, then divide and spread the egg–black bean mixture evenly over the crusts. Sprinkle each with ½ cup cheese. Sprinkle with a bit of oregano. Bake each pizza for another 10–15 minutes, separately. Remove from the oven and let cool for 5 minutes.

5. Cut each pizza into four slices. Garnish with pickled jalapeño slices and crema if desired.

Egg and Ham Casserole

Submitted by Colleen Padilla, ClassyMommy.com. This casserole is so easy to make, the kids can help. And with the kid-friendly combination of ham, eggs, and Cheddar, they will gobble it right up!

INGREDIENTS | SERVES 12

4 slices gluten-free white bread, cubed

¼ pound ham, diced

¼ cup diced green bell peppers (optional)

8 large eggs

¾ cup shredded Cheddar cheese

1. Preheat oven to 350°F.

2. Lightly grease a 9" × 13" baking dish. Arrange the bread cubes in the bottom of the prepared pan.

3. Layer the ham and peppers on top. (You can also add any other favorite veggies or meats you'd like to include.)

4. In a medium bowl, whisk the eggs. Pour the eggs over the top and sprinkle with the cheese.

5. Cover with foil and bake immediately for 30–35 minutes, or refrigerate overnight to bake in the morning for breakfast.

Seasoned Chili Corn Bread Skillet

Submitted by Angela England, UntrainedHousewife.com. This one-skillet dish is super simple to make. It goes from stove to oven to table with zero fuss.

INGREDIENTS | SERVES 8

1 pound ground beef

1 garlic clove, minced

½ cup chopped yellow onion

1 red bell pepper, thinly sliced

1 (27-ounce) can chili beans in sauce

2 teaspoons Cajun seasoning

2 packages gluten-free corn muffin mix, such as Bob's Red Mill

1 cup shredded sharp Cheddar cheese, divided

½ cup water

3 large eggs

1. Preheat oven to 350°F.

2. Brown the ground beef in an ovenproof skillet over medium-high heat, about 8–10 minutes. Add the garlic, onion, and red pepper. Cook until soft, about 5–8 minutes. Add the chili beans and stir. Continue to cook as you prepare the corn bread batter.

3. In a bowl, combine the Cajun seasoning, corn mix, half the cheese, water, and eggs. Pour the corn bread batter over the chili bean mixture in the skillet and transfer to the oven. Bake for 30–35 minutes, until a knife inserted into the center comes out clean.

4. Let it cool slightly, then flip it over onto a large, round plate and sprinkle the rest of the shredded cheese over the top. Slice and eat.

CHAPTER 6

Muffins, Scones, and Biscuits

Blueberry Muffins

These blueberry muffins are best when you pile the batter high and sprinkle with sugar before baking.

INGREDIENTS | YIELDS 12

½ cup butter, room temperature

1 cup granulated sugar, plus extra for topping

2 eggs, lightly beaten

2 cups gluten-free all-purpose flour

2 teaspoons baking powder

½ teaspoon salt

1 teaspoon xanthan gum

½ cup whole milk

1 teaspoon pure vanilla extract

1½ cups wild Maine blueberries, washed and drained

1. Preheat oven to 375°F. Line 12 muffin cups with liners.

2. In a large mixing bowl, cream the butter and sugar together using a wooden spoon. Add the eggs one at a time, beating well after each addition.

3. In a separate bowl, sift together the flour, baking powder, salt, and xanthan gum. Slowly whisk the dry ingredients into the egg mixture along with the milk and vanilla. Fold in the blueberries.

4. Spoon into the prepared muffin tin, piling the batter high. Sprinkle with sugar. Bake for 25–30 minutes or until a toothpick inserted in the center of a muffin comes out clean. Serve warm.

Banana Nut Muffins

Submitted by Jessie Weaver, VanderbiltWife.com. Coconut flour is high in fiber and is a good source of protein. You only need small amounts to bake a whole batch of goodies, although you need a lot of eggs to work with it. It's a very "thirsty" flour!

INGREDIENTS | YIELDS 12

1 ripe banana

¼ cup butter, melted

¼ cup whole milk

6 large eggs

6 packed tablespoons light brown sugar

2 tablespoons water

½ teaspoon vanilla extract

½ teaspoon salt

½ cup coconut flour

½ teaspoon baking powder

1½ teaspoons ground cinnamon

½ cup pecan pieces

1. Preheat oven to 400°F. Line 12 muffin cups with liners.

2. In a mixing bowl, mash together the banana and melted butter. Add the milk, eggs, brown sugar, water, and vanilla and mix well.

3. In a separate bowl, whisk together the salt, coconut flour, baking powder, and cinnamon. Add to wet ingredients and stir to incorporate. Fold in the pecan pieces.

4. Scoop into the prepared muffin tin, filling the cups ¾ full. Bake for 20–22 minutes or until a toothpick inserted in the center of a muffin comes out clean. Cool on wire racks.

Chocolate Chip Pecan Pumpkin Muffins

Submitted by Heather Holtz, RunEatPlayBlog.com. Almond flour is one of the better gluten-free baking flours because of its taste and texture. It is also high in protein.

INGREDIENTS | YIELDS 12

1 cup almond flour
1 teaspoon baking soda
½ teaspoon salt
1 teaspoon ground cinnamon
½ teaspoon ground nutmeg
½ teaspoon pumpkin pie spice
½ cup chopped pecans
1 cup canned pumpkin
2 large eggs
1 teaspoon pure vanilla extract
2 tablespoons almond butter
2 tablespoons honey
½ cup chocolate chips
½ cup pumpkin seeds for topping (optional)

1. Preheat oven to 350°F. Line 12 muffin cups with liners.

2. In a mixing bowl, mix together the almond flour, baking soda, salt, cinnamon, nutmeg, pumpkin pie spice, and chopped pecans.

3. In a separate mixing bowl, whisk together the pumpkin, eggs, vanilla, almond butter, and honey. Slowly whisk the dry ingredients into the wet ingredients. Stir in the chocolate chips.

4. Spoon into the prepared muffin tin, filling the cups ¾ full. Top with pumpkin seeds, if using. Bake for 20–25 minutes or until a toothpick inserted in the center of a muffin comes out clean.

Almond Flour vs. Almond Meal

Almond flour and almond meal are often used interchangeably, but typically almond meal is not ground quite as fine. It doesn't usually matter which you use in most recipes, however some recipes require an extra-fine flour. Almond flour is recommended for this recipe.

Glazed Lemon Poppy Seed Muffins

These traditional muffins taste fresh and delicious. The secret is the lemonade concentrate.

INGREDIENTS | YIELDS 12

2 cups gluten-free all-purpose flour

¼ cup granulated sugar

1 heaping tablespoon poppy seeds

½ tablespoon lemon zest (optional)

3 teaspoons baking powder

½ teaspoon salt

1 teaspoon xanthan gum

½ cup plus 2 tablespoons whole milk

½ cup lemonade concentrate, thawed

⅓ cup butter, melted

1 large egg, slightly beaten

1 cup powdered sugar

2 teaspoons fresh lemon juice

Lemon Simple Syrup

If you prefer not to use lemonade concentrate, you can make your own! Simply combine ¾ cup granulated sugar with 1 cup water in a medium saucepan and boil on high until the sugar is dissolved (stir frequently). Remove from the heat and allow it to cool. Then add 2 teaspoons fresh lemon juice and stir until combined.

1. Preheat oven to 400°F. Line 12 muffin cups with liners.

2. In a large mixing bowl, whisk together the flour, sugar, poppy seeds, lemon zest (if using), baking powder, salt, and xanthan gum.

3. Add ½ cup milk, lemonade concentrate, butter, and egg. Beat until just combined.

4. Spoon the batter into the muffin cups. Use all the batter between the 12 muffin cups; these don't rise a lot so you want them full. Bake for 25–30 minutes or until a toothpick inserted in the center of a muffin comes out clean. Cool on wire racks until just warm, 10–15 minutes.

5. While the muffins cool, combine the powdered sugar, 2 tablespoons milk, and lemon juice. While they're still warm but not fragile, dip the tops of the muffins in the glaze and return to the cooling rack.

Doughnut Muffins

These muffins have the flavor of a cinnamon doughnut without all the fuss!

INGREDIENTS | YIELDS 12

1 large egg

½ cup whole milk

⅓ cup plus 1 tablespoon butter, melted

1½ cups gluten-free all-purpose flour

2 teaspoons baking powder

½ teaspoon salt

½ teaspoon xanthan gum

1 tablespoon plus ½ teaspoon ground cinnamon

¼ teaspoon ground nutmeg

½ cup granulated sugar

1 tablespoon honey

1. Preheat oven to 350°F. Line 12 muffin cups with liners.

2. In a small bowl, beat the egg with a fork. Add the milk and ⅓ cup melted butter and stir.

3. Add the flour, baking powder, salt, xanthan gum, ½ teaspoon cinnamon, nutmeg, and sugar and stir until just mixed. Scoop the batter into the prepared muffin tin, filling the cups ¾ full.

4. In a separate bowl, mix together 1 tablespoon melted butter, 1 tablespoon ground cinnamon, and 1 tablespoon honey. Spoon over the muffins. Bake for 15–20 minutes or until a toothpick inserted in the center of a muffin comes out clean. Cool on wire racks.

Morning Glory Muffins

Submitted by Melissa Jennings, StockpilingMoms.com. These nutritious muffins with carrots, almonds, and coconut are a great way to start your morning!

INGREDIENTS | YIELDS 24

3 large eggs

¾ cup coconut oil

¾ cup whole milk

1 teaspoon vanilla extract

2 cups gluten-free all-purpose flour

¾ teaspoon xanthan gum

1 packed cup light brown sugar

2 teaspoons baking soda

2 teaspoons ground cinnamon

½ teaspoon salt

2 medium carrots, peeled and shredded

½ cup shredded, unsweetened coconut

½ cup raisins

½ cup slivered almonds

1. Preheat oven to 350°F. Line 24 muffin cups with liners.

2. In a large mixing bowl, beat the eggs, coconut oil, milk, and vanilla on medium speed for 1 minute.

3. Add the flour, xantham gum, brown sugar, baking soda, cinnamon, and salt. Beat until just combined.

4. Fold in the carrots, coconut, raisins, and almonds.

5. Spoon the batter into the prepared muffin tin, filling each about ½ full. Bake for 20 minutes or until a toothpick inserted in the center of a muffin comes out clean. Cool on wire racks.

Spiced Pear Muffins

These spiced pear muffins make the perfect addition to a fall brunch.

INGREDIENTS | YIELDS 24

2 large eggs
½ cup butter, melted
½ cup unsweetened applesauce
1 teaspoon vanilla extract
3 cups gluten-free all-purpose flour
2 cups granulated sugar, plus extra for sprinkling
2 teaspoons baking soda
1 teaspoon ground cinnamon
¼ teaspoon ground ginger
¼ teaspoon ground nutmeg
2 teaspoons xanthan gum
½ teaspoon salt
4 cups chopped, peeled ripe pears
1 cup chopped pecans (optional)

1. Preheat oven to 350°F. Line 24 muffin cups with liners.

2. In a large mixing bowl, beat the eggs, butter, applesauce, and vanilla on medium speed for 1 minute.

3. Add the flour, sugar, baking soda, cinnamon, ginger, nutmeg, xanthan gum, and salt. Beat until just combined.

4. Fold in the pears, and pecans, if using.

5. Spoon the batter into the muffin tin, filling each cup about ⅔ full. Sprinkle the tops with sugar. Bake for 25–30 minutes or until a toothpick inserted in the center of a muffin comes out clean. Cool on wire racks.

Perfect Rounded Muffin Tops Every Time!

To get those perfectly smooth, rounded muffin tops, use an ice cream scoop with a trigger to scoop the batter into the muffin cups.

Peanut Butter Banana Chocolate Chip Muffins

This recipe has been adapted from Lindsay Frank, www.PandorasDeals.com. These muffins are delicious, moist, and tasty and they use applesauce instead of oil or butter so there's no added fat.

INGREDIENTS | YIELDS 24

1½ cups gluten-free all-purpose flour

1 teaspoon baking powder

1 teaspoon baking soda

1 teaspoon xanthan gum

½ teaspoon salt

¼ cup granulated sugar

¼ packed cup light brown sugar

¼ cup applesauce

1 large egg

2 ripe bananas, mashed

½ cup creamy peanut butter

1 teaspoon vanilla extract

1 cup mini chocolate chips, plus 2 tablespoons for topping

1. Preheat oven to 350°F. Grease 24 mini muffin cups or line with cupcake liners.

2. In a medium bowl combine the flour, baking powder, baking soda, xanthan gum, and salt. Use a whisk or fork to stir until mixed.

3. In a large mixing bowl, combine the sugars and applesauce. Add the egg and beat to combine. Add the dry ingredients and mix until just combined.

4. Add the mashed bananas, peanut butter, and vanilla. Mix until just combined. Stir in 1 cup of chocolate chips by hand.

5. Spoon the batter into the muffin tins. Press extra chocolate chips into the tops of muffins if desired. Bake for 10–12 minutes or until a toothpick comes out clean. Allow to cool in the muffin tins for 3–5 minutes, then gently remove to a cooling rack until completely cool. Store in an airtight container.

Paleo Gingerbread Muffins

Submitted by Kamila Gornia, SensualAppealBlog.com, these Paleo-friendly gingerbread muffins are gluten- and dairy-free. Because of the blackstrap molasses, they pack a great nutritional punch. If you prefer sweeter muffins, you can use dark molasses instead of blackstrap.

INGREDIENTS | YIELDS 12

1 cup almond flour
¼ cup coconut flour
½ cup potato starch
3 teaspoons ground ginger
3 teaspoons pumpkin pie spice
1 teaspoon baking soda
4 large eggs, room temperature
⅓ cup blackstrap molasses
⅓ cup maple syrup
¼ cup extra-virgin unrefined coconut oil, melted
1 teaspoon vanilla extract

1. Preheat oven to 350°F. Line a muffin tray with 12 cupcake/muffin liners and spray it with cooking oil to prevent sticking.

2. In a large bowl, mix together the flours, starch, ginger, pie spice, and baking soda. In a small bowl, mix together all of the remaining ingredients.

3. Add the wet ingredients to the dry ingredients and whisk together until incorporated.

4. Distribute the batter evenly among the liners. Bake for 15–20 minutes or until a toothpick inserted in the center of a muffin comes out clean. Cool before eating.

Pumpkin Orange Muffins

The flavors of pumpkin and orange blend together for a refreshing burst of flavor in these moist and delicious muffins.

INGREDIENTS | YIELDS 18

2 large eggs
⅓ cup butter, melted
⅓ cup orange juice
1 cup canned pumpkin
1¾ cups gluten-free all-purpose flour
3 teaspoons pumpkin pie spice
1 teaspoon baking soda
½ teaspoon baking powder
½ teaspoon salt
1 teaspoon xanthan gum
1½ cups granulated sugar, plus extra for topping

1. Preheat oven to 350°F. Grease 18 muffin cups.

2. In a large mixing bowl, beat the eggs, butter, orange juice, and pumpkin on medium speed for 1 minute. Add the remaining ingredients and stir to combine.

3. Spoon the batter into the muffin cups, filling each about ¾ full. Sprinkle the tops with sugar. Bake for 25–30 minutes or until a toothpick inserted in the center of a muffin comes out clean. Cool on wire racks.

Traditional Buttermilk Biscuits

Light handling is the secret to making these fluffy, flaky biscuits!

INGREDIENTS | YIELDS 15

4 cups gluten-free all-purpose flour

4 teaspoons baking powder

½ teaspoon baking soda

2 teaspoons salt

½ cup Crisco shortening

1½ cups buttermilk

Oils and Shortenings

Not all shortenings are gluten free. When in doubt, it is always best to check with the manufacturer to be sure.

1. Preheat oven to 450°F.

2. In a large bowl, combine the flour, baking powder, baking soda, and salt.

3. Add the shortening and use a pastry blender or two knives to cut the shortening into the dry ingredients until the mixture resembles fine crumbs. You do not want big chunks of shortening.

4. Add the buttermilk and stir to combine.

5. Knead the dough 10–20 times on a lightly floured surface and roll it out until it's about ½" thick. Don't over-handle the dough.

6. Use a biscuit cutter to cut into 3" circles and place them in an ungreased 9" × 13" baking pan. It is okay if they touch slightly, but don't crowd the pan.

7. Bake for 10–15 minutes or until golden brown on top; serve warm with butter and your favorite condiment (honey, molasses, apple butter, jam, or sausage gravy).

Italian Cheddar Biscuits

These savory biscuits go well with eggs or an omelet or as an addition to your brunch menu.

INGREDIENTS | YIELDS 15

1½ cups warm water

1 (16-ounce) package Bob's Red Mill Gluten Free Pizza Crust Whole Grain Mix

2 large eggs, lightly beaten

6 tablespoons olive oil, divided

1 cup shredded sharp Cheddar cheese

1¼ cups shredded pecorino Romano or Parmesan cheese, divided

3 tablespoons Italian seasoning, divided

1 teaspoon salt

¼ teaspoon ground black pepper

1. In a large bowl, combine the water and yeast from the packet included in the pizza mix box. Allow the yeast to proof for 5–10 minutes.

2. Add the pizza mix, eggs, 2 tablespoons olive oil, Cheddar cheese, 1 cup pecorino Romano cheese, 2 tablespoons Italian seasoning, salt, and pepper; blend thoroughly. Cover and allow the dough to rise for 30 minutes.

3. Meanwhile, preheat oven to 400°F. Grease a half sheet pan. In a small bowl, blend the remaining 4 tablespoons olive oil with 1 tablespoon Italian seasoning.

4. Form the dough into balls (about ¼ cup of dough per biscuit) and place on the prepared pan; moisten your hands to keep the dough from sticking.

5. Use a pastry brush to spread the seasoned olive oil mixture on top of each roll. Top with a pinch of the reserved pecorino Romano.

6. Bake for 20 minutes or until golden brown on top; serve warm with butter.

Ham and Swiss Biscuits

The ham and Swiss cheese add protein to a traditional biscuit. These make for a quick breakfast on the go, or they make a nice accompaniment to eggs!

INGREDIENTS | YIELDS 18

2 cups gluten-free all-purpose flour

2 teaspoons baking powder

½ teaspoon baking soda

½ teaspoon xanthan gum

½ cup butter, chilled

2 ounces ham, minced

2 ounces Swiss cheese, shredded

⅔ cup buttermilk

1. Preheat oven to 450°F and grease a large rimmed 12" × 18" baking sheet.

2. In a large bowl, combine the flour, baking powder, baking soda, and xanthan gum.

3. Add the butter and use a pastry blender or two knives to cut into the dry ingredients until the mixture resembles fine crumbs.

4. Add the ham, cheese, and buttermilk. Stir to combine. If it's too wet, add a bit more flour until it no longer sticks to your hands.

5. Knead the dough 10–20 times on a lightly floured surface and roll it out until it's about ½" thick. Don't over-handle the dough.

6. Use a biscuit cutter to cut into circles and place them on the prepared baking sheet. It is okay if they touch slightly, but don't crowd the pan.

7. Bake for 10–15 minutes or until golden brown on top.

Cream Scones

These delicious scones are super easy to put together and taste great with mini chocolate chips or currants.

INGREDIENTS | YIELDS 8

2 cups gluten-free all-purpose flour

⅓ cup granulated sugar, plus 2 tablespoons for topping

1 tablespoon baking powder

½ teaspoon salt

1 teaspoon xanthan gum

1¼ cups heavy cream, plus extra for topping

⅓ cup dried currants or mini chocolate chips

Scone School

Scones were traditionally made in Scotland with unleavened oats and baked on a griddle. Now they are usually made of flour and baked in the oven. Scones became popular in England in the early 1800s and are often served with tea. We use gluten-free all-purpose flour and xanthan gum to make this delicious gluten-free version of a classic scone.

1. Preheat oven to 425°F and place a rack in the top third of the oven.

2. In a medium mixing bowl, whisk together the flour, sugar, baking powder, salt, and xanthan gum.

   Add the heavy cream and stir gently until the dry ingredients are moistened. If it's too sticky, you can add another ¼ cup flour. Be careful not to over-handle the dough. Fold in the currants or chocolate chips.

3. Turn onto a floured mat and gently roll the dough into a circle that is about 1" thick. Brush with more heavy cream and sprinkle with sugar.

4. Cut into 8 triangles and place them 1" apart on an ungreased baking sheet. Bake until golden brown, 12–15 minutes.

Raspberry Scones

This recipe was submitted by Jeremy Dabel of WholesomeDinnerTonight.blogspot.com. The white beans add a nice texture to these gluten-free scones. You can substitute any of your favorite frozen fruits for the raspberries to get a different flavor.

INGREDIENTS | YIELDS 12

2 tablespoons chilled unsalted butter

½ cup granulated sugar

1 large egg

1 teaspoon vanilla extract

⅔ cup puréed white beans (puréed in a blender until smooth)

2 cups gluten-free old-fashioned rolled oats (such as Bob's Red Mill)

¼ teaspoon salt

1 cup gluten-free all-purpose flour

½ cup frozen raspberries

Surprise Ingredient: Puréed White Beans

Dried white beans that have been cooked in the slow cooker and puréed are a wonderful addition to just about any baked good, adding fiber, antioxidants, lowering the fat, and adding great texture to gluten-free recipes. You can use the bean purée 1:1 to replace half the fat in most recipes. Give it a try!

1. Preheat oven to 350°F. Line a baking sheet with parchment paper.

2. In a large mixing bowl, cream the butter and sugar together with an electric mixer on medium-high speed for about 1 minute. Add the egg, vanilla, and bean purée and mix on medium-low speed for 2 minutes.

3. In a separate bowl, whisk together the oats, salt, and flour.

4. With the mixer on low speed, add the dry ingredients slowly, by the cup, to the bean mixture. Once combined, add the raspberries and mix only enough to combine.

5. Use an ice-cream scoop to drop the batter onto the prepared baking sheet. Bake for 20 minutes, until slightly golden brown and set. Cool on wire racks.

Oatmeal Raisin Scones

The oats add a nice texture to these hearty scones.

INGREDIENTS | YIELDS 16

1 cup gluten-free all-purpose flour

½ cup gluten-free old-fashioned rolled oats (such as Bob's Red Mill)

1 teaspoon baking powder

¼ teaspoon baking soda

¼ teaspoon salt

½ teaspoon xanthan gum

¼ cup chilled butter

½ cup raisins

½ cup buttermilk

1 cup powdered sugar

½ teaspoon vanilla

1–2 tablespoons milk

1. Preheat oven to 425°F and place a rack in the top third of the oven.

2. In a medium mixing bowl, whisk together the flour, oats, baking powder, baking soda, salt, and xanthan gum.

3. Using a pastry blender or two knives, cut the butter into the flour mixture until it resembles crumbs. Stir in the raisins. Add the buttermilk and mix into a soft dough. Split the dough in half.

4. Turn half the dough onto a floured mat and knead until smooth. Gently roll the dough into a circle that is about ¾" thick. Cut into 8 triangles and place them 1" apart on an ungreased baking sheet. Repeat with the second half. Bake until golden brown, 12–15 minutes. Cool on wire racks.

5. In a small bowl, mix sugar, vanilla, and 1 tablespoon milk. Add more milk, a few drops at a time, until a thin icing forms. Drizzle cooled scones with icing.

Chocolate Doughnuts

These doughnuts aren't too terribly sweet so they make a fun and guilt-free breakfast treat! Decorate them for any occasion to make them extra festive.

INGREDIENTS | YIELDS 12

2 large eggs

1 cup whole milk

2 tablespoons butter, melted

2 cups gluten-free all-purpose flour

¼ cup cocoa powder

½ cup granulated sugar

1 teaspoon baking powder

½ teaspoon baking soda

1½ cups semisweet chocolate chips, divided

Sprinkles, toasted coconut, or nuts for toppings (optional)

1. Preheat oven to 325°F. Grease doughnut pans with butter.

2. In a large mixing bowl, whisk together the eggs, milk, and butter.

3. Add the flour, cocoa powder, sugar, baking powder, and baking soda. Whisk to combine. Fold in ½ cup chocolate chips.

4. Spoon the batter into the doughnut pans, filling each well about half full. Bake for 12–15 minutes or until the tops of the doughnuts feel firm and cooked through (touch them lightly). Remove them from the oven, cool for 3–5 minutes in the pan, then remove to wire racks and cool completely.

5. While the doughnuts cool, place the remaining cup of chocolate chips in a double broiler (or set a glass bowl over a pan of boiling water) and allow them to melt slowly. Spread the melted chocolate on each doughnut, then sprinkle with your favorite topping.

Cinnamon Doughnuts

These doughnuts are wonderfully soft and chewy . . . just like a cake doughnut should be!

INGREDIENTS | YIELDS 12

2 cups gluten-free all-purpose flour

2¼ cups granulated sugar, divided

2 teaspoons baking powder

2 teaspoons ground cinnamon, divided

½ teaspoon ground nutmeg

½ teaspoon salt

1 teaspoon xanthan gum

10 tablespoons butter, divided

1 large egg, beaten

1¼ cups buttermilk

2 teaspoons pure vanilla extract

1. Preheat oven to 350°F. Grease doughnut pans with butter.

2. In a large bowl, whisk together the flour, 1¼ cups sugar, baking powder, 1 teaspoon cinnamon, nutmeg, salt, and xanthan gum.

3. Melt the butter in a small bowl. In another small bowl, whisk together the egg, buttermilk, and 2 tablespoons melted butter. Pour the wet ingredients into the dry and mix until just combined.

4. Spoon the batter into a large resealable bag and cut a corner. Squeeze the batter into the wells of the doughnut pan until they're ¾ full.

5. Bake for 15–18 minutes, until golden brown and firm to the touch. Cool in the pan for 3–5 minutes, then remove to a wire rack.

6. Combine the remaining tablespoon cinnamon and 1 cup sugar in a small bowl. When the doughnuts are cool enough to touch, dip each doughnut first into the remaining melted butter until coated on both sides and then into the cinnamon on both sides. Place them on a plate to serve.

Glazed Pumpkin Doughnuts

Try these for your next Thanksgiving breakfast.

INGREDIENTS | YIELDS 12

2 cups gluten-free all-purpose flour

½ cup granulated sugar

1½ teaspoons baking powder

¼ teaspoon baking soda

½ teaspoon salt

1½ teaspoons pumpkin pie spice

1 teaspoon xanthan gum

1 cup pumpkin purée

1 tablespoon molasses such as Grandma's Molasses

2 large eggs

½ cup buttermilk

¼ cup butter, melted

1½ cups powdered sugar

2 tablespoons whole milk

1 teaspoon vanilla extract

1. Preheat oven to 325°F. Grease doughnut pans with butter.

2. In a large bowl, whisk together the flour, sugar, baking powder, baking soda, salt, pumpkin pie spice, and xanthan gum.

3. In a smaller bowl, whisk together the pumpkin purée, molasses, eggs, buttermilk, and butter. Pour the wet ingredients into the dry and mix until just combined.

4. Spoon the batter into a large resealable bag and cut a corner. Squeeze the batter into the wells of the doughnut pan until they're ¾ full.

5. Bake for 12–15 minutes, until golden brown and firm to the touch. Cool in the pan for 3–5 minutes, then remove to a wire rack.

6. To make the glaze, combine the powdered sugar, milk, and vanilla in a small bowl and whisk until smooth. When the doughnuts are cool enough to touch, dip the top of each doughnuts in the glaze. Return to the rack to cool completely.

Apple Cider Doughnuts

These apple cider doughnuts will bring back childhood memories of apple picking and hay rides!

INGREDIENTS | YIELDS 12

2 cups gluten-free all-purpose flour
1¼ cups granulated sugar, divided
1½ teaspoons baking powder
¼ teaspoon baking soda
1 teaspoon salt
3 teaspoons ground cinnamon, divided
¼ teaspoon ground nutmeg
1 teaspoon xanthan gum
½ cup plus 2 tablespoons apple cider
2 large eggs
½ cup buttermilk
2 tablespoons butter, melted
1 cup powdered sugar

1. Preheat oven to 325°F. Grease doughnut pans with butter.

2. In a large bowl, whisk together the flour, ¾ cup granulated sugar, baking powder, baking soda, salt, 1 teaspoon cinnamon, nutmeg, and xanthan gum.

3. In a smaller bowl, whisk together ½ cup apple cider, the eggs, buttermilk, and melted butter. Pour the wet ingredients into the dry and mix until just combined.

4. Spoon the batter into a large resealable bag and cut a corner. Squeeze the batter into the wells of the doughnut pan until they're ¾ full.

5. Bake for 18–20 minutes, until golden brown and firm to the touch. Cool in the pan for 3–5 minutes, then remove to a wire rack.

6. To make the glaze, combine the powdered sugar with 2 tablespoons apple cider in a small bowl and whisk until smooth. Set out another bowl with the remaining ½ cup sugar mixed with the remaining 2 teaspoons cinnamon.

7. When the doughnuts are cool enough to touch, dip the top of each doughnut in the glaze, then sprinkle with cinnamon sugar. Return to the rack to cool completely.

Browned Butter Glazed Spice Doughnuts

Adapted with permission from Laura Franklin, BetterinBulk.com. These muffins are delicious, moist, and tasty and they use applesauce instead of oil or butter, so there's no added fat.

INGREDIENTS | YIELDS 6

¼ cup buttermilk

1 large egg, beaten

2 teaspoons butter, melted

1 cup gluten-free all-purpose flour

⅓ cup granulated sugar

1 teaspoon baking powder

1 teaspoon xanthan gum

⅛ teaspoon ground nutmeg

⅛ teaspoon ground cinnamon

½ teaspoon salt

Browned Butter Glaze (see sidebar)

Browned Butter Glaze

Melt ¼ cup butter in a small saucepan over low heat until browned. Pour into a bowl and add 1 cup powdered sugar, 2 tablespoons milk, and ½ teaspoon vanilla extract. Whisk until smooth.

1. Preheat oven to 325°F. Lightly grease a doughnut pan.

2. In a small bowl, stir together the buttermilk, egg, and butter. Mix together all the remaining ingredients except the glaze in a medium bowl. Add the wet ingredients to the bowl with the dry ingredients and stir until fully mixed.

3. Spoon the batter into a large resealable bag and cut a corner. Squeeze the batter into the wells of the doughnut pan until they're ¾ full. Bake for 10 minutes or until lightly browned.

4. Cool in the pan on top of the oven for a few minutes before removing. Dip each doughnut in the Browned Butter Glaze and set on a plate until the glaze has set.

Corn Bread Doughnuts

These savory doughnuts can be served alone, with a smear of butter or cream cheese, or split and used to encase eggs, breakfast meats, and/or cheese. Or serve under sausage gravy.

INGREDIENTS | YIELDS 6

⅞ cup yellow cornmeal

2 tablespoons gluten-free all-purpose flour

1 teaspoon baking powder

½ teaspoon baking soda

2 teaspoons granulated sugar

½ teaspoon salt

1 large egg, lightly beaten

1 cup buttermilk

1 tablespoon melted butter

1. Preheat oven to 425°F. Grease a doughnut pan.

2. In a large bowl, stir together the cornmeal, flour, baking powder and soda, sugar, and salt.

3. In a small bowl, whisk together the egg and buttermilk. Slowly drizzle in the melted butter, whisking constantly. Add the wet ingredients to the dry and stir to combine. The batter will be a bit runny.

4. Spoon the batter into the prepared doughnut pan. Bake for 10 minutes or until the tops begin to turn golden brown and the doughnuts feel firm to the touch. Cool on a wire rack.

CHAPTER 7

Breads and Breakfast Loaves

Banana Bread

*Make sure to use very ripe bananas when making banana bread
or muffins. It makes all the difference in the world!*

INGREDIENTS | SERVES 12

4 large eggs

2 cups mashed very ripe banana (about
4 bananas)

1 cup granulated sugar

½ cup unsweetened applesauce

⅓ cup melted butter

1 teaspoon pure vanilla extract

1½ cups brown rice flour

½ cup sorghum flour

1 teaspoon baking soda

½ teaspoon salt

½ cup walnuts and/or chocolate chips
(optional)

1. Preheat oven to 350°F. Grease a 9" × 5" loaf pan
   with butter.

2. In a large mixing bowl, beat the eggs lightly. Add the
   bananas, sugar, applesauce, melted butter, and vanilla
   and mix thoroughly.

3. Add the flours, baking soda, and salt to the wet
   ingredients. Mix until just combined. Fold in the nuts
   and/or chocolate chips if using.

4. Spread the batter into the prepared loaf pan. (It will be
   thick.) Bake for 60–75 minutes. Tent with a piece of
   aluminum foil if it starts to get too brown on top. It is
   done when a toothpick inserted in the center comes
   out clean. Allow the bread to rest for 10 minutes before
   removing to a rack to cool completely.

Chocolate Chip Zucchini Bread

You will never know that there are vegetables in this yummy bread or that it's gluten-free. It's a perfect way to sneak vegetables into snacks for those picky children!

INGREDIENTS | SERVES 12

2 large eggs

½ cup granulated sugar

½ cup melted butter

½ cup unsweetened applesauce

1 tablespoon vanilla extract

1 cup brown rice flour

½ cup almond flour

½ cup cornstarch

1 teaspoon xanthan gum

½ teaspoon baking soda

¼ teaspoon baking powder

½ teaspoon salt

1 tablespoon ground cinnamon

¼ teaspoon ground cloves

¼ teaspoon ground nutmeg

1½ cups fresh shredded zucchini

½ cup chocolate chips

1. Preheat oven to 350°F. Grease a 9" × 5" loaf pan with butter.

2. In a large mixing bowl, beat together the eggs, sugar, butter, and applesauce. Add the vanilla and mix well.

3. In a separate bowl, combine the flours, cornstarch, xanthan gum, baking soda, baking powder, salt, cinnamon, cloves, and nutmeg.

4. Add the dry ingredients to the wet ingredients and mix well.

5. Add the zucchini and chocolate chips and stir to combine.

6. Pour the batter into the prepared loaf pan and bake for 60–70 minutes or until a toothpick inserted in the center comes out clean.

Overwhelmed with Zucchini

Zucchini always seems to yield a plentiful harvest! If you find yourself overwhelmed with zucchini, these zucchini pancakes are a great way to use up extra zucchini. You may also want to try the Zucchini Pancakes in Chapter 8.

Pumpkin Bread

Always a fan favorite, this moist and flavorful gluten-free version of the traditional holiday bread is good enough to fool even the harshest critic. Best with an add-in such as nuts, raisins, or chocolate chips.

INGREDIENTS | SERVES 12

4 large eggs
1 (15-ounce) can pumpkin purée
1 cup granulated sugar
½ cup unsweetened applesauce
⅓ cup melted butter
1 teaspoon pure vanilla extract
1½ cups brown rice flour
½ cup coconut flour
½ cup sorghum flour
1 teaspoon ground cinnamon
½ teaspoon ground cloves
1 teaspoon baking soda
½ teaspoon salt
½ cup walnuts, raisins, or chocolate chips (you can use up to 1 cup total; this bread is very good with ½ cup walnuts and ½ cups raisins or chocolate chips)

1. Preheat oven to 350°F. Grease a 9" × 5" loaf pan with butter.

2. In a large mixing bowl, beat the eggs lightly. Add the pumpkin, sugar, applesauce, melted butter, and vanilla and mix thoroughly.

3. Add the flours, cinnamon, cloves, baking soda, and salt to the wet ingredients. Mix until just combined. Fold in the nuts/raisins/chocolate chips.

4. Spread the batter into the prepared loaf pan. (It will be thick.) Bake for 60–75 minutes. Tent with a piece of aluminum foil if it starts to get too brown on top. It is done when a toothpick inserted in the center comes out clean. Allow the bread to rest for 10 minutes before removing to a rack to cool completely.

The Muffin Alternative

Any quick bread recipe can easily be adapted to muffins. One loaf equals about 12 muffins. Reduce the bake time to 15–20 minutes.

Lemon Bread

Submitted by Melissa Jennings, StockpilingMoms.com. Serve this delicious lemon bread with lemon curd, jam, or even clotted cream. It freezes well too! Perfect for company or yourself with hot tea.

INGREDIENTS | SERVES 12

1 cup butter, room temperature
1 cup granulated sugar
1 cup almond flour
½ cup coconut flour
5 large eggs, beaten
Grated rind and juice from 1 lemon

1. Preheat oven to 350°F. Grease a 9" × 5" loaf pan with butter.

2. Combine all the ingredients in a mixing bowl and mix thoroughly. Pour into the prepared loaf pan. Bake for 35–45 minutes or until golden brown and firm to the touch. Cool on a wire rack.

Grain-Free Blueberry Banana Nut Sticky Bread

Submitted by Lindsay Cotter, CotterCrunch.com, this grain-free sticky bread is nutrient-dense and delicious. Perfect for recovery after a long run.

INGREDIENTS | SERVES 12

¼ cup coconut flour
¼ cup almond flour (or gluten-free all-purpose flour)
½ teaspoon baking powder
½ teaspoon cream of tartar
2 scoops whey vanilla protein powder
2 tablespoons nut/fruit trail mix
1 small ripe banana
1 large egg
2 tablespoons original unsulphured molasses
4 ounces blueberry Greek yogurt
1 teaspoon liquid stevia (optional)
1 tablespoon butter or coconut oil

1. Preheat oven to 350°F. Grease a glass 9" × 9" pan with butter.

2. In large a bowl, mix the flours, baking powder, cream of tartar, protein powder, and trail mix. Set aside.

3. In a small bowl, mash the banana and egg; blend with the dry ingredients. Add the molasses, yogurt, and stevia; mix again.

4. Pour into a greased bread pan and bake for 20 minutes. Remove from oven and pour the melted butter or coconut oil on top; let it cool. This bread does not rise; it's a thin batter and the bread has a sticky middle, which tastes amazing.

Cranberry Oat Bread

Submitted by Jessie Weaver, VanderbiltWife.com. This bread is the perfect mix of tangy and sweet. It is great served immediately or frozen for later use.

INGREDIENTS | SERVES 8–10

1¼ cups gluten-free all-purpose flour

1 cup gluten-free oat bran

⅓ cup granulated sugar

1 tablespoon baking powder

½ teaspoon ground cinnamon

½ teaspoon xanthan gum

¼ teaspoon salt

1¼ cups applesauce

2 large whole eggs, lightly beaten

1 egg white, lightly beaten

¼ cup melted butter

1½ teaspoons vanilla extract

½ cup dried cranberries

½ cup chopped walnuts

1. Preheat oven to 350°F. Butter an 8" × 4" loaf pan.

2. In a large mixing bowl, blend the flour, oat bran, sugar, baking powder, cinnamon, xanthan gum, and salt.

3. In a separate bowl, blend the applesauce, eggs, egg whites, butter, and vanilla. Stir the wet ingredients into the dry ingredients and fold in the cranberries and walnuts.

4. Spread the batter into the prepared loaf pan and bake for 50–55 minutes, or until a toothpick inserted in the center comes out clean. Cool in the pan for 10 minutes before removing to a wire rack to cool completely. Slice and serve immediately, or wrap tightly and store for up to 24 hours or freeze for later use.

Refrigerate or Freeze?

Gluten-free baked goods tend to dry out faster than their glutinous counterparts. For most of these breads and cakes, it is best to freeze if you don't plan to serve within 24 hours. You generally don't need to store them in the refrigerator. In fact, the refrigerator sometimes causes them to dry out faster than they would at room temperature. Always wrap and seal tightly when not in use

Apple Cider "Coffee Cake" Bread

Submitted by Lindsay Cotter, CotterCrunch.com. This gluten-free and grain-free "bread" is a sweet and sour buttery delight.

INGREDIENTS | SERVES 8–10

1 cup almond flour

¼ cup coconut flour

¼ teaspoon salt

½ tablespoon combination of nutmeg, ginger, and clove

½ teaspoon cream of tartar

½ teaspoon baking powder

50 grams vanilla protein powder (about 2 scoops)

2 large eggs, gently beaten

⅓ cup unsweetened applesauce

3 tablespoons honey

1 ounce dried apples, chopped

2 tablespoons raw apple cider vinegar

1 tablespoon melted butter or coconut oil

1. Preheat oven to 350°F. Butter a 9" × 9" baking pan.

2. In a large bowl, blend the flours, salt, spices, cream of tartar, baking powder, and protein powder; set aside.

3. In a separate bowl, whisk the egg and fold in the dry ingredients. Add the applesauce, honey, dried apple, and vinegar; stir to combine.

4. Spread the batter into the prepared pan and bake for 15–18 minutes or until set. Drizzle with melted butter or coconut oil and let it cool. This bread is lightly sour and sweet. If you want it sweeter, add more honey. Serve with yogurt or cream cheese.

Benefits of Apple Cider Vinegar

Apple cider vinegar is a fermented product made from crushed and aged apples, and it's a lifesaver when it comes to gut health and immunity. It aids digestion and it can also help ease heartburn and acid reflux.

Mini Banana Chocolate Chip Loaves

Submitted by Jessica Cohen, EatSleepBe.com. These gluten- and dairy-free mini loaves make nice holiday gifts and are perfect for mornings on the go.

INGREDIENTS | SERVES 8–10

2 cups gluten-free prepared muffin mix (such as Glutino)

1 teaspoon ground cinnamon

2 large eggs, lightly beaten

1 cup coconut milk

¼ cup safflower oil

½ teaspoon pure vanilla extract

1½ cups mashed banana

½ cup mini chocolate chips (Enjoy Life brand is dairy-free)

1. Preheat oven to 350°F. Grease 8 mini loaf pans.

2. In a large mixing bowl, combine the muffin mix and cinnamon. In a separate bowl, mix together the eggs, coconut milk, oil, vanilla, and bananas. Add the wet mixture to the dry ingredients and mix thoroughly. Fold in the chocolate chips

3. Spread the batter evenly into the prepared loaf pans and bake for 20 minutes, or until a toothpick inserted in the center comes out clean. Cool in the pan for 10 minutes before removing to a wire rack to cool completely.

Apple Cinnamon Breakfast Bars

Another great grab-and-go breakfast, perfect for busy mornings. Kids gobble these up!

INGREDIENTS | YIELDS 12

1½ cups whole milk

1 cup almond butter (or your favorite nut butter)

1 teaspoon vanilla extract

½ cup unsweetened applesauce

½ cup maple syrup

2 cups grated apple (liquid squeezed out)

2 large eggs, lightly beaten

3 cups gluten-free old-fashioned rolled oats (such as Bob's Red Mill)

½ cup gluten-free all-purpose flour

2 teaspoons baking soda

2 teaspoons ground cinnamon

1. Preheat oven to 350°F. Grease a glass 9" × 13" baking pan with butter.

2. Stir together the milk, almond butter, vanilla, applesauce, maple syrup, apple, and eggs in a large mixing bowl. Add the remaining ingredients and stir to combine. Spread in the prepared baking pan and bake for 35–40 minutes. Cool completely before cutting.

Corn Bread

Traditionally made with bacon drippings in a cast-iron skillet, this sweeter version of corn bread is made with butter and baked in the oven. It is delicious with butter. Also try topping it with honey or molasses for a yummy treat.

INGREDIENTS | SERVES 8–10

1¾ cups gluten-free all-purpose flour

1 cup cornmeal

¼ cup granulated sugar

2 teaspoons baking powder

¼ teaspoon baking soda

1 teaspoon xanthan gum

½ teaspoon salt

1¼ cups whole milk

½ cup melted butter, cooled

1 large egg, gently beaten

1. Preheat oven to 375°F. Butter a 9" × 9" baking pan or round 9" cake pan.

2. In a large bowl, blend the flour, cornmeal, sugar, baking powder, baking soda, xanthan gum, and salt.

3. In a separate bowl, whisk together the milk, butter, and egg. Stir the wet ingredients into the dry ingredients and mix until just combined.

4. Spread the batter into the prepared pan and bake for 20–25 minutes or until the edges begin to pull away from the sides of the pan and it's beginning to brown on top. Allow the corn bread to cool 5–10 minutes before cutting, and serve warm.

Raspberry Yogurt Bundt Cake

This recipe comes from Colleen Kennedy, SouffleBombay.com. You can use fresh-squeezed orange juice in addition to or in place of water for the drizzle in this recipe.

INGREDIENTS | SERVES 12

3 cups plus 1 teaspoon gluten-free all-purpose flour, divided

1½ teaspoons baking powder

2 teaspoons xanthan gum

⅛ teaspoon salt

1 cup butter, room temperature

1¾ cups granulated sugar

2 tablespoons fresh-squeezed orange juice

1 teaspoon grated orange zest

3 large eggs

1 cup vanilla yogurt

2½ cups fresh raspberries

Drizzle

1 cup powdered sugar

1 tablespoon or more of water

1. Preheat oven to 350°F. Grease Bundt pan.

2. Combine 3 cups flour with the baking powder, xanthan gum, and salt in a medium bowl and set aside.

3. In a large bowl, combine the butter and sugar and beat with a mixer until creamy. Beat in the orange juice and zest. Add the eggs one at a time, beating after each addition. Add the yogurt and mix until blended.

4. Add the dry ingredients and mix until just blended. Toss the berries gently with 1 teaspoon of flour; add to the batter.

5. Spoon the batter into the prepared pan. Bake for 60–65 minutes or until a toothpick inserted comes out clean. Cool for 30 minutes; remove from pan.

6. For the drizzle, combine the powdered sugar and water; add more sugar or water to reach desired consistency if necessary. Drizzle over the cake.

Blueberry Breakfast Cake

This moist, buttery blueberry cake with a zing of lemon is utterly divine! It uses gluten-free all-purpose flour, so you don't have to keep a stock of gluten-free flours in your pantry.

INGREDIENTS | SERVES 9

½ cup unsalted butter, room temperature

¾ cup granulated sugar, plus 1 tablespoon for topping

1 teaspoon lemon zest

1 large egg, room temperature

1 teaspoon vanilla extract

2 cups gluten-free all-purpose flour

1 teaspoon xanthan gum

2 teaspoons baking powder

1 teaspoon salt

½ cup buttermilk

2 cups frozen Maine blueberries, thawed

Homemade Buttermilk

To make homemade buttermilk, place 1 tablespoon of vinegar or lemon juice in a liquid measuring cup. Fill with milk until it reaches the 1-cup line. Let stand for 5 minutes.

1. Preheat oven to 350°F. Grease an 8" × 8" square pan with butter.

2. In a large mixing bowl, cream the butter and sugar until light and fluffy. Add the lemon zest, egg, and vanilla and beat for 1 minute.

3. In a separate bowl, combine the flour, xanthan gum, baking powder, and salt.

4. Add the dry ingredients to the wet ingredients alternately with the buttermilk, beginning and ending with the flour mixture. The batter will be thick.

5. Gently fold in the blueberries. Pour into the prepared pan and bake for 40–50 minutes or until a toothpick inserted in the center comes out clean.

Jewish Apple Cake

This moist, dense cake is perfect for company or a church potluck. When wrapped carefully, it keeps well for days. Traditionally, Jewish Apple Cake is made with vegetable oil, but this buttery version takes the flavor factor up a notch!

INGREDIENTS | SERVES 12

2 cups gluten-free all-purpose flour

1 teaspoon baking soda

1 teaspoon xanthan gum

2 teaspoons ground cinnamon

½ teaspoon salt

1 cup butter, melted

2 cups granulated sugar

2 large eggs

1 teaspoon pure vanilla extract

4 cups peeled and thinly sliced McIntosh (or other sweet) apples

1 tablespoon powdered sugar for topping

1 cup heavy cream, whipped to form soft peaks

1. Preheat oven to 350°F. Grease a 9" × 13" baking pan with butter.

2. In a small bowl, combine the flour, baking soda, xanthan gum, cinnamon, and salt. Set aside.

3. In a large mixing bowl, combine the butter, sugar, eggs, and vanilla and mix well. Add the dry ingredients slowly and mix until combined. Fold in the apples.

4. Spread the batter into the prepared pan. Bake for 45–50 minutes or until a toothpick inserted in the center comes out clean.

5. Cool cake in pan for 25–30 minutes. Top individual servings with powdered sugar and whipped cream.

Presentation Is Everything!

For a pretty presentation, try layering the apples and the batter, starting with a layer of apples on the bottom, ½ the cake batter, another layer of apples, the remaining ½ cake batter, and topping with the remaining apples. Sprinkle with cinnamon sugar and bake as directed.

Cinnamon Streusel Coffee Cake

Always a favorite breakfast treat, this gluten-free version of cinnamon streusel coffee cake is moist and delicious. If you don't have a tube pan, you can use a 9" × 13" baking pan.

INGREDIENTS | SERVES 12

1 cup butter, divided

1 cup granulated sugar

2 large eggs

1 teaspoon vanilla extract

1 cup sour cream

2 cups gluten-free all-purpose flour

1 teaspoon baking powder

1 teaspoon baking soda

1 teaspoon xanthan gum

3 teaspoons ground cinnamon, divided

¼ teaspoon salt

1 packed cup light brown sugar

1 cup chopped walnuts

Tube Pan vs. Bundt Pan

A Bundt pan and a tube pan can usually be used interchangeably. A tube pan has flat sides and is generally used for sponge cakes and angel food cake. A Bundt pan is a type of tube pan with a rounded bottom and fancier fluted edges. For this recipe, you may use either.

1. Preheat oven to 350°F. Butter and flour a tube pan.

2. In a large mixing bowl, cream ¾ cup softened butter and granulated sugar until light and fluffy. Add the eggs, one at a time, beating well after each addition. Add the vanilla and sour cream and blend.

3. Add the flour, baking powder, baking soda, xanthan gum, 1 teaspoon cinnamon, and salt and mix just until blended.

4. To make the streusel, melt ¼ cup butter and mix with the brown sugar, 2 teaspoons cinnamon, and the chopped walnuts in a small bowl.

5. Spread half the batter into the pan, sprinkle with half the streusel mixture, spread the rest of the batter on top of that, and finish with remaining streusel. Bake for 50–55 minutes or until a toothpick inserted in the center comes out clean. Allow to cool for 10–15 minutes, then remove to a rack or serving plate to cool completely. Slice and serve or wrap tightly to store for up to 24 hours.

Lemon Yogurt Cake

Submitted by Jeremy Dabel, WholesomeDinnerTonight.blogspot.com. The raspberries are the perfect complement to this tangy lemon cake, and the sugary glaze adds an extra layer of sweet goodness.

INGREDIENTS | SERVES 10–12

3 large eggs

¾ cup butter, room temperature

1½ cups granulated sugar

Zest of 1½ lemons

1½ teaspoons pure vanilla extract

1½ cups plain yogurt

2½ cups plus 2 tablespoons Pamela's Baking and Pancake Mix

3 tablespoons fresh lemon juice

1½ cups powdered sugar

Raspberries for topping (optional)

1. Preheat oven to 350°F. Grease 2 (9") round cake pans with butter.

2. Separate the yolks from the eggs. Reserve the yolks in a small dish and add the egg whites to the bowl of an electric mixer. Whip the egg whites on high speed using the whisk attachment until stiff peaks form (5–10 minutes). Gently transfer to another bowl and set aside.

3. Cream the butter and sugar together in the electric mixer on high speed using the paddle attachment until creamy, about 1 minute. Add the egg yolks one at a time at medium-low speed. Add the lemon zest and vanilla.

4. Slowly add ¼ of the yogurt, then ¼ the baking mix, and repeat until all the yogurt and baking mix have been added and the batter is combined. Fold in the whipped egg whites by hand using a spatula; gently combine with as little stirring as possible.

5. Pour the batter equally into the cake pans. Level the batter by gently shaking the pan back and forth. Let the batter rest in the pans at room temperature for 5 minutes.

6. Bake for 25–30 minutes or until a toothpick inserted in the center comes out clean. Cool in the pans for at least 20 minutes.

7. Meanwhile, prepare the glaze by mixing the lemon juice and powdered sugar in a small bowl with a whisk until the glaze is runny. Remove the cakes from the pans and spread ⅓ the glaze on top of one. Stack the other cake on top of the glazed cake. Pour the rest of the glaze over the top of the stacked cakes. Arrange raspberries on top to cover the top of the cake if desired.

Raspberry Streusel Breakfast Squares

If you need a grab-and-go breakfast, look no further than these buttery raspberry delights! They also pack well in a lunchbox.

INGREDIENTS | YIELDS 12

1½ cups plus 2 tablespoons gluten-free all-purpose flour, divided

1 cup firmly packed dark brown sugar, divided

1¼ cups gluten-free old-fashioned rolled oats (such as Bob's Red Mill)

¾ teaspoon salt

¾ teaspoon baking powder

½ teaspoon baking soda

1½ teaspoons ground cinnamon, divided

13 tablespoons chilled butter, divided

1 tablespoon lemon juice

1 (10-ounce) bag frozen raspberries

1. Preheat oven to 350°F. Grease a glass 9" × 13" baking pan with butter.

2. Combine 1½ cups flour, ¾ cup brown sugar, rolled oats, salt, baking powder, baking soda, and ½ teaspoon cinnamon in a food processor. Add 12 tablespoons butter (in chunks) and pulse until crumbly.

3. Reserve 1 cup of the streusel mixture in a small bowl for the topping. Spread the rest in the buttered pan and pat down to form a crust. Bake for 12 minutes or until lightly brown on top. Remove from the oven and let cool.

4. Place the remaining 2 tablespoons flour, ¼ cup brown sugar, and 1 teaspoon cinnamon in a bowl and mix with a fork. Add 1 tablespoon melted butter, lemon juice, and raspberries and gently toss together until the raspberries are coated with the mixture. Spread the raspberry mixture on top of the cooled crust.

5. Sprinkle the remaining streusel topping on top of the raspberries and bake for 35–40 minutes or until light brown on top. Cool completely before cutting.

Blueberry Peach Breakfast Cake

This delicious seasonal dish is easy to whip up and it's always a crowd pleaser!

INGREDIENTS | SERVES 12

½ cup butter

1½ cups gluten-free all-purpose flour

1 cup granulated sugar

2 teaspoons baking powder

½ teaspoon salt

½ teaspoon xanthan gum

1½ cups whole milk

3 cups sliced fresh peaches

1 cup fresh blueberries

1. Preheat oven to 350°F. Place the butter in a 9" × 13" baking pan and put it in the oven. Remove from the oven as soon as the butter is melted.

2. Meanwhile, in a medium mixing bowl, combine the flour, sugar, baking powder, salt, and xanthan gum. Then whisk in the milk until it makes a smooth batter.

3. Pour the batter over the melted butter in the baking pan. Spread the fruit over the batter. Bake until the top is golden brown and bubbly, 50–60 minutes. Serve warm or at room temperature. Refrigerate the leftovers.

Oatmeal Raisin Breakfast Bars

Homemade breakfast bars are a great grab-and-go breakfast option to have on hand for those busy mornings. For an extra-yummy treat, replace raisins with mini chocolate chips.

INGREDIENTS | YIELDS 12

1 cup melted butter, cooled

2 large eggs, lightly beaten

1 cup granulated sugar

2 cups gluten-free all-purpose flour

2 cups gluten-free old-fashioned rolled oats (such as Bob's Red Mill)

½ teaspoon baking powder

½ teaspoon salt

1 cup raisins

1. Preheat oven to 350°F. Butter a 9" × 13" baking pan.

2. In a large mixing bowl, whisk together the butter, eggs, and sugar. Add the flour, oats, baking powder, and salt and stir until blended. Fold in the raisins.

3. Spread the batter into the prepared baking dish. Bake for 20–25 minutes or until set and starting to brown on top. Cool before cutting. These freeze well if you want to wrap them individually to have for future breakfasts. They also make a nutritious after-school snack.

Fruit Pizza (Chapter 15)

Southwestern Breakfast Taco (Chapter 4)

Oatmeal Raisin Scones (Chapter 6)

Mexican-Style Breakfast Pizza (Chapter 5)

Blackberry French Toast Casserole (Chapter 12)

Country Sweet Potato Breakfast Hash (Chapter 5)

Raspberry Streusel Breakfast Squares (Chapter 7)

Eggs Florentine (Chapter 12)

Flourless Breakfast Oatmeal Cookies (Chapter 7)

Veggie Cheese Frittata (Chapter 3)

Traditional Buttermilk Biscuits (Chapter 6)

Apple, Pear, and Banana Green Smoothie
(Chapter 13)

Zucchini Pancakes (Chapter 8)

Salted Caramel Mocha Latte (Chapter 14)

Breakfast Salad (Chapter 11)

Jewish Apple Cake (Chapter 7)

Caramelized Pear Parfait (Chapter 15)

Hash Brown Breakfast Casserole (Chapter 5)

Spiced Pear Muffins (Chapter 6)

Berry Banana Baked Oatmeal (Chapter 10)

Cherry Tomatoes on the Side (Chapter 11)

Nutella Waffles with Strawberries (Chapter 9)

Herbed Baked Eggs for One (Chapter 2)

Chocolate Doughnuts (Chapter 6)

Flourless Breakfast Oatmeal Cookies

Submitted by Lisa Douglas, CrazyAdventuresinParenting.com. These soft, gooey breakfast cookies are flourless, made with oatmeal, and a kid favorite!

INGREDIENTS | YIELDS ABOUT 24 COOKIES

3 ripe bananas, mashed

⅓ cup unsweetened applesauce

⅛ cup ground flaxseed (optional)

2 cups gluten-free quick-cooking rolled oats

¼ cup whole milk

1 tablespoon granulated sugar

1 tablespoon honey

1 teaspoon pure vanilla extract

1 teaspoon ground cinnamon

½ teaspoon ground nutmeg

½ cup raisins, dried fruit, or nuts (optional)

1. Preheat oven to 350°F. Grease a cookie sheet.

2. Combine the mashed bananas and applesauce in a large bowl. Add the rest of the ingredients and mix thoroughly. Let it stand for at least 5 minutes, until the oatmeal begins to soak up the mixture and expands a bit.

3. Spoon heaping tablespoons of the dough onto the prepared cookie sheet; sprinkle with additional cinnamon if desired. Bake for 15–20 minutes, until browned slightly on top. Allow the cookies to set for 5 minutes before removing to a wire rack to cool completely.

Pumpkin Breakfast Cookies

Submitted by Jessica Lieb, TheBKeepsUsHonest.com, these breakfast cookies are super simple and easy to change up just by simply using different fillings—nuts, seeds, dried fruit, chocolate chips, etc.

INGREDIENTS | YIELDS ABOUT 12 COOKIES

½ cup almond butter

½ cup pumpkin purée

¼ cup pure maple syrup

1 large egg

1 teaspoon pure vanilla extract

½ teaspoon baking soda

½ teaspoon ground cinnamon

¼ teaspoon salt

Filling: ½ cup of your choice of dried fruits, nuts, seeds, coconut, etc.

1. Preheat oven to 350°F.

2. Mix together all the ingredients except the filling. Fold in the filling.

3. Place tablespoon-size scoops of the dough on the prepared cookie sheet. Bake for 15–18 minutes or until the edges start to turn brown.

CHAPTER 8

Pancakes and Crepes

Corn Crepes
150

Mini Strawberry Buckwheat
Shortcakes with Strawberry
Coconut Cream
151

Corn Crepes with Salmon and
Cream Cheese
152

Bacon, Egg, and Cheese Crepes
152

Basic Pancakes

Top these basic pancakes with anything from maple syrup to fresh fruit.

INGREDIENTS | YIELDS 16

½ cup whole milk

2 large eggs

1½ tablespoons butter, melted

1 tablespoon baking powder

1 cup rice flour

Flour Substitutions

Try substituting rice or potato flour in some recipes; chickpea flour also makes an excellent savory pancake.

1. In the bowl of a food processor, mix together the milk, eggs, and butter. Slowly add the baking powder and flour.

2. Heat a griddle pan or large frying pan to medium. Drop about a teaspoon of butter on it and when the butter sizzles, pour the batter on the griddle in about 2"-diameter circles.

3. When bubbles come to the top, turn the pancakes and continue to fry until golden brown, about 2–3 minutes per side. Place on a plate in a warm oven while you make the others.

Easy Paleo Pancake

This pancake recipe is quick and easy and can be multiplied to make enough for an entire family. Once cooked, sprinkle the pancake with cinnamon or a small amount of agave nectar for an old-fashioned pancake taste.

INGREDIENTS | YIELDS 1

1 banana

1 large egg

1 teaspoon nut butter of choice

2 teaspoons coconut oil

Bananas as Thickeners

Bananas can be a good replacement for flour. Bananas act as thickening agents in recipes that would normally be too fluid.

1. In a small bowl, mash the banana with a fork. Beat the egg and add to the banana. Add the nut butter and mix well.

2. Lightly coat a frying pan or griddle with the oil and heat on medium. Pour all the pancake mixture onto the preheated pan. Cook until lightly brown on each side, about 2 minutes per side.

Red Velvet Pancakes

This recipe comes together quickly because it uses a prepared gluten-free pancake mix; Pamela's Baking and Pancake Mix is recommended.

INGREDIENTS | YIELDS 12–15

2 cups Pamela's Gluten-Free Baking and Pancake Mix

2 tablespoons granulated sugar

2 tablespoons unsweetened cocoa

1¼ cups whole milk

1½ teaspoons red gel food color

2 large eggs

Easy Cream Cheese Topping (see sidebar)

Powdered sugar and berries for garnish

Easy Cream Cheese Topping

Beat 4 ounces softened cream cheese, ¼ cup softened butter, and 3 tablespoons whole milk with an electric mixer until creamy. Slowly beat in 2 cups powdered sugar and blend until smooth.

1. Combine the dry ingredients in a medium mixing bowl.

2. Whisk the wet ingredients together in a liquid measuring cup. Pour the wet ingredients into the dry and whisk to combine.

3. Allow the pancake batter to sit for 10–20 minutes. It will be on the runny side. If you like a thicker pancake, you can reduce the milk to 1 cup.

4. Meanwhile, heat an electric griddle to 375°F. Brush the griddle with butter and spoon the pancake batter onto the hot griddle using a trigger ice-cream scoop. Cook the pancakes until bubbles form and the edges begin to look dry. Flip them and cook for 1 more minute. Stack the pancakes 2 or 3 high on dinner plates.

5. Cut off a tiny corner of a resealable bag and drizzle the pancakes with frosting. Sprinkle with powdered sugar and garnish with your favorite berries.

Millet Buckwheat Pancakes

Submitted by Jeremy Dabel of WholesomeDinnerTonight.blogspot.com. It is written so you can make a double batch of the dry ingredients and save half to use at a later time.

INGREDIENTS | YIELDS 35–40 (3–4") PANCAKES

2 cups white rice flour

1 cup buckwheat flour

2½ cups millet flour

¾ cup tapioca starch

1¾ teaspoons sea salt

6 teaspoons baking powder

2 tablespoons olive oil

1 large egg

1½ tablespoons granulated sugar

¼ cup unsweetened applesauce

2¼ cups water

Make Ahead for Easy Mornings!

Mix the dry ingredients in a large batch ahead of time to speed things up on those busy mornings.

1. In a large bowl, mix together the flours, tapioca starch, salt, and baking powder until well combined. Divide the mixture in half and save half of the dry mix for another day.

2. In a medium bowl, whisk together the olive oil, egg, sugar, applesauce, and water.

3. Add half of the dry ingredient mixture to the wet ingredient mixture; stir to combine.

4. Preheat a flat griddle over medium heat and grease with a light coating of coconut oil or butter for every other batch of pancakes. Spoon the pancake batter onto the hot griddle, approximately ¼ cup at a time. Cook for about 1 minute on each side or until just golden brown. Flip.

5. Stack the pancakes in a pile so they can soften from the steam; this makes them moist and just chewy enough that you won't know they are gluten-free.

Oatmeal Pancakes

These pancakes have the flavor of a traditional pancake made with white flour, but the oatmeal lends a pleasant texture and makes them extra special. Soaking the oats overnight makes this grain easier to digest.

INGREDIENTS | YIELDS 10–12 PANCAKES

2 cups gluten-free old-fashioned rolled oats (such as Bob's Red Mill)

½ cup brown rice flour (any gluten-free flour will work)

2 cups buttermilk

2 medium eggs, beaten

2 tablespoons melted coconut oil or butter

2 tablespoons granulated sugar

1 teaspoon baking powder

1 teaspoon baking soda

½ teaspoon salt

½ teaspoon ground cinnamon

⅓ cup whole milk (optional)

1. The night before you want to serve these pancakes for breakfast, combine the oats, flour, and buttermilk in a large glass bowl. Stir well. Cover with plastic wrap and set overnight.

2. The next morning, add the eggs, oil, sugar, baking powder, baking soda, salt, and cinnamon to the bowl and stir together. Add milk if you need to make them the proper consistency. The batter shouldn't be runny, but it should be thin enough to allow pancakes to form when placed on a griddle.

3. Let the pancake batter set while you preheat a griddle to medium heat and lightly coat with butter or oil. Spoon the pancake batter onto the hot griddle, approximately ¼ cup at a time. Flip when the tops are bubbly and puffed up and they look slightly dry around the edges, about 2 minutes. Flip them again and cook for 1 more minute. Remove to a plate and serve with toppings of your choice. They're wonderful with butter and maple syrup, or try them with jam or fresh fruit.

Pumpkin Pancakes

These pancakes are delicious with whipped cream on top. They are sweet and decadent and maybe a bit more dessert than breakfast, but who's counting?

INGREDIENTS | YIELDS 8–10 PANCAKES

2 large eggs

1 cup canned pumpkin purée

1¼ cups whole milk

2 tablespoons melted butter

2 cups gluten-free all-purpose flour

2 teaspoons baking powder

1 teaspoon pumpkin pie spice

½ teaspoon salt

3 packed tablespoons light brown sugar

1. In a medium bowl, beat the eggs lightly. Add the pumpkin, milk, and butter and whisk together.

2. Add the remaining ingredients; mix well. Add more milk if needed for a pancake-like consistency.

3. Heat a griddle to medium-high heat or 375°F and lightly coat with coconut oil or butter. Spoon the pancake batter onto the hot griddle, approximately ¼ cup at a time. Cook until bubbly in the middle and dry around the edges, about 2 minutes. Flip and continue cooking until browned on both sides and cooked through, about 1 more minute. Serve with butter and maple syrup or top with whipped cream.

Flourless Pumpkin Pancakes

Submitted by Alexandra Maul, MadetoGlow.com. This pumpkin pancake recipe is perfect for those who prefer to eat grain-free, and the flaxseed is a great source of fiber and omega-3 fatty acids.

INGREDIENTS | YIELDS 4 PANCAKES

⅓ cup canned pumpkin purée

2 large eggs

2 tablespoons ground flaxseed

2 tablespoons melted butter

1 teaspoon pure vanilla extract

½ teaspoon pumpkin pie spice

¼ teaspoon ground cinnamon

2 teaspoons honey or maple syrup

¼ teaspoon salt

1. Whisk together all the ingredients in a medium mixing bowl until smooth.

2. Heat a griddle to medium-high heat or 375°F and lightly coat with coconut oil or butter. Spoon the pancake batter onto the hot griddle, approximately ¼ cup at a time. Cook for 2–3 minutes or until bubbly in the middle and dry around the edges. Flip and continue cooking for 1–2 minutes or until cooked through. Serve with butter and maple syrup.

Peach Pancakes

Peaches are in season during the late summer and early fall, but you can enjoy these peach pancakes all year round by using canned peaches. If using canned peaches, make sure to drain out all the juice before dicing.

INGREDIENTS | YIELDS 12–14 PANCAKES

2 large eggs

2½ cups buttermilk

¼ cup melted butter

2½ cups gluten-free all-purpose flour

2 teaspoons baking powder

1 teaspoon baking soda

1 teaspoon salt

2 tablespoons granulated sugar

½ teaspoon ground cinnamon

¼ teaspoon ground ginger

2 cups diced peaches, fresh or canned

Additional peach slices for garnish

Make Better Pancakes

Pancakes as well as most baked goods are best when you start with room-temperature ingredients. They also turn out better when the batter is allowed to rest for 10–30 minutes before cooking.

1. In a mixing bowl, beat the eggs lightly. Add the buttermilk and melted butter and whisk together.

2. Add the dry ingredients and mix well. Gently fold in the peaches and let the batter sit for 10–15 minutes.

3. Heat a griddle to medium-high heat or 375°F and lightly coat with coconut oil or butter. Spoon the pancake batter onto the griddle, approximately ¼ cup at a time. Cook until bubbly and dry around the edges. Flip and continue cooking until browned on both sides and cooked through. Press down gently to make sure the batter cooks thoroughly. Stack them on a plate, garnish with peach slices, and serve with butter and powdered sugar or maple syrup.

Blueberry-Banana Blender Pancakes

These pancakes are quick to put together because you mix all the ingredients in a blender and pour!

1 cup whole milk

2 tablespoons melted butter

1 teaspoon pure vanilla extract

1 tablespoon honey

½ cup mashed ripe bananas

2 cups gluten-free old-fashioned rolled oats (such as Bob's Red Mill)

½ teaspoon ground cinnamon

¼ teaspoon salt

1½ teaspoons baking powder

1 extra-large egg

½ cup wild Maine blueberries (you can get these in the freezer section: keep a bag on hand for baking purposes)

1. Place all the ingredients except the egg and blueberries in a blender; blend until smooth. Add the egg and pulse until incorporated.

2. Heat a griddle to medium-high heat or 375°F and lightly coat with coconut oil or butter. Pour the pancake batter onto the hot griddle, making each pancake 3–4" in diameter. Sprinkle each with a scant tablespoon of blueberries. Cook until bubbly and dry around the edges. Flip and continue cooking for 1–2 more minutes, until cooked through. Serve with butter and maple syrup.

Wild vs. Cultivated Blueberries

Blueberries are one of the few fruits indigenous to the United States. There are two basic types of blueberries. Lowbush blueberries grow in the wild, primarily in Maine, Novia Scotia, Quebec, and New Brunswick. They are smaller and sweeter than their cultivated counterpart, the highbush blueberry, which is bred for size and isn't usually as flavorful. "Wild Maine blueberries" are of the lowbush variety and are generally preferred for use in baked goods such as pies, pancakes, and muffins. They have a very short (two-week) harvest season, but fortunately you can buy them canned or frozen to enjoy year-round.

Strawberry Shortcake Pancakes

Strawberries are sweetest when they are local and in season. If you can't find local seasonal strawberries, look for berries that are a deep red in color and give them a sniff. If they smell like strawberries, they are more likely to be fresh and close to their peak.

INGREDIENTS | YIELDS 6–8 PANCAKES

1 large egg
1¼ cups buttermilk
2 teaspoons butter, melted
1¼ cups gluten-free all-purpose flour
1 teaspoon baking powder
½ teaspoon baking soda
½ teaspoon salt
1 tablespoon granulated sugar
¼ teaspoon ground cinnamon
1 cup small-diced fresh strawberries
2 cups sweetened whipped cream
Additional strawberries for garnish

1. In a large mixing bowl, beat the egg lightly. Add the buttermilk and melted butter and whisk together.

2. Add the dry ingredients and mix well. Gently fold in the strawberries and let the batter sit for 10–15 minutes.

3. Heat a griddle to medium-high heat or 375°F and lightly coat with coconut oil or butter. Spoon the pancake batter onto the hot griddle, approximately ¼ cup at a time. Cook until they bubble in the middle and look dry around the edges, about 2–3 minutes. Flip and continue cooking until browned on both sides and cooked through, 2–3 more minutes. Press down gently to make sure the batter cooks thoroughly around the berries.

4. Stack 3 or 4 pancakes per plate, spreading a layer of whipped cream between each. Top each stack with a dollop of whipped cream and a strawberry half.

Carrot Cake Pancakes

Submitted by Lisa Douglas, CrazyAdventuresinParenting.com. This fantastic pancake recipe uses no flour and has the benefit of added protein. The carrot and pumpkin flavors taste delicious paired together.

INGREDIENTS | YIELDS 4

¼ cup vanilla protein powder

½ cup vanilla Greek yogurt

1 teaspoon ground cinnamon

½ teaspoon ground ginger

½ teaspoon ground nutmeg

½ teaspoon pumpkin pie spice

¼ teaspoon ground cloves

½ teaspoon baking powder

1 large egg

1¼ cups gluten-free old-fashioned rolled oats

½ cup pumpkin purée

¼ cup water

1 tablespoon honey

½ teaspoon pure vanilla extract

2 tablespoons granulated sugar

½ cup finely minced carrots

¼ cup grated carrots

1. Combine all the ingredients except the carrots in a blender. Blend until well mixed. If the batter is too thick, add additional water to reach desired consistency. Add most of the finely minced carrots (reserve 1–2 tablespoons for garnish) and pulse until incorporated. Fold in the grated carrots and stir until well mixed.

2. Heat a griddle to medium-high heat or 375°F and lightly coat with coconut oil or butter. Spoon the pancake batter onto the hot griddle, approximately ¼ cup at a time. Cook until the sides are browned and a spatula can slide under easily. Flip and cook for another 1–2 minutes. Serve with Cream Cheese Frosting Syrup (see sidebar), if desired.

Cream Cheese Frosting Syrup

In a small bowl, blend ½ cup warm cream cheese, ¼ cup maple syrup, and 1 teaspoon cinnamon-sugar with a whisk until clumps are gone. Drizzle on top of each pancake and sprinkle with minced carrot for garnish.

Coconut Flour Pancakes

Cooking with gluten-free flours can be intimidating, but the sweet taste of coconut flour in these pancakes proves that even gluten-free pancakes can be delicious.

INGREDIENTS | YIELDS 8 PANCAKES

2 large whole eggs

2 egg whites

3 tablespoons butter

3 tablespoons whole milk

1½ teaspoons maple syrup

1 teaspoon sea salt

3 tablespoons coconut flour

½ teaspoon baking powder

1 teaspoon ground cinnamon

1 teaspoon ground allspice

⅓ cup ground flaxseed

1 teaspoon vanilla extract

1. In a large bowl, use a wire whisk to mix together the eggs and egg whites, butter, milk, maple syrup, and salt.

2. Add the coconut flour and baking powder, whisking until thoroughly mixed. Add the cinnamon, allspice, flaxseed, and vanilla. Stir to combine thoroughly.

3. Heat a skillet over medium heat with just enough butter to coat lightly.

4. Spoon 2–3 tablespoons of batter onto the skillet, making the pancakes about 3–4" in diameter. Cook for 3–5 minutes, turning once.

Zucchini Pancakes

These savory zucchini pancakes make a nutritious, albeit slightly unconventional, breakfast. Serve them with a side of bacon or sausage for extra protein. (They're also a great side dish for dinner.)

INGREDIENTS | YIELDS 6–8 PANCAKES

2 medium zucchini, shredded (about 2 cups)

2 cloves garlic, minced

2 tablespoons coconut flour

3 large eggs, lightly beaten

4 ounces Parmesan cheese, grated

1 teaspoon salt

¼ teaspoon ground black pepper, or to taste

2 tablespoons olive oil or butter

2 tablespoons sour cream

1 tablespoon chopped parsley

1. Shred the zucchini (a food processor is ideal for this) and squeeze dry with a dishtowel or paper towels. Dump it into a medium mixing bowl and add the minced garlic, flour, eggs, cheese, salt, and pepper. Mix lightly with a fork. If it seems too wet to hold together, you can add another tablespoon coconut flour.

2. Heat the olive oil or butter in a cast-iron skillet over medium heat. Using an ice-cream scoop or serving spoon, drop the zucchini mixture into the pan in little blobs and flatten a bit with the fork. Cook until browned, 3–4 minutes, and then flip. Cook another 2–3 minutes or until desired doneness and transfer to paper towels to drain.

3. Top pancakes with sour cream and parsley before serving.

Maple Bacon German Pancakes

Submitted by Laura Franklin, BetterInBulk.net, this is a fun variation on plain German pancakes.

INGREDIENTS | SERVES 2

2 tablespoons butter

2 tablespoons maple syrup

2 slices bacon, cooked and crumbled

2 large eggs

½ cup gluten-free all-purpose flour

½ cup whole milk

¼ teaspoon salt

1. Preheat oven to 400°F. Place the butter in a 9" pie pan and melt in the oven as it preheats; remove from the oven and swirl the butter around so that the bottom and sides of the dish are covered. Drizzle the syrup in the pan and sprinkle with crumbled bacon. Set aside.

2. In a small mixing bowl, beat the eggs with a whisk. Beat in the flour, milk, and salt, just until mixed. Pour into the pie plate.

3. Bake for 25–30 minutes or until puffy and golden brown. Serve immediately with powdered sugar or maple syrup.

Dutch Babies with Peaches

Submitted by Michele Reneau, RealFoodRealtor.com. This an easy way to make "pancakes" in one dish, and this recipe is packed with protein instead of a bunch of simple carbohydrates that will leave you hungry in an hour. If you wish, you can mix the ingredients in a blender.

INGREDIENTS | SERVES 4

⅓ cup butter

8 large eggs

¼ cup coconut flour, sifted

⅓ cup arrowroot flour

1 cup coconut milk

½ teaspoon salt

1 medium peach, sliced

½ cup maple syrup, divided

1. Preheat oven to 425°F.

2. Place butter in a 9" × 13" pan and allow it to melt in the oven.

3. In a large bowl, whisk the eggs. Add the flours, milk, and salt; mix well.

4. Pour the batter in the hot pan with the melted butter; bake for 20–25 minutes.

5. Serve with sliced peaches and a drizzle of maple syrup.

Lemon Ricotta Pancakes

Submitted by Trina O'Boyle, OboyOrganic.com. The ricotta and stiff egg whites makes these pancakes light and fluffy.

INGREDIENTS | SERVES 4

1 cup gluten-free ricotta cheese such as Organic Valley

1 cup whole milk

3 large eggs, separated

¼ cup granulated sugar

Zest and juice of 1 lemon

1½ cups gluten-free all-purpose flour

1 tablespoon baking powder

¼ teaspoon salt, divided

2 tablespoons flaxseed meal

1. In a large bowl, whisk together the ricotta, milk, egg yolks, sugar, lemon zest, and lemon juice until smooth.

2. In a separate bowl, mix together the flour, baking powder, ⅛ teaspoon salt, and flaxseed meal; pour over the ricotta mixture. Stir until just combined.

3. In another large bowl, beat the egg whites until frothy. Add the remaining ⅛ teaspoon salt and continue beating until soft peaks form. Using a rubber spatula, fold ⅓ of the egg whites into the ricotta mixture.

4. Preheat a griddle over medium heat and lightly coat with oil or butter. Spoon the batter on the griddle, ¼ cup at a time. Cook until bubbles form on top and the pancakes are golden brown underneath, 1–2 minutes. Flip the pancakes and cook for 1 minute more. Transfer to a plate.

Butternut Squash Pancakes

This recipe comes from Elle, a blogger at WeCanBegintoFeed.blogspot.com. This is a great way to use up leftover butternut squash from dinner. It's a hearty breakfast that will keep you satisfied until lunch.

INGREDIENTS | YIELDS 6–8 PANCAKES

2 large eggs

2 tablespoons almond flour

½ cup cooked and mashed butternut squash

2 teaspoons coconut flour

½ teaspoon ground cinnamon

3 tablespoons almond milk, divided

About Using Coconut Flour

Coconut flours vary, so the amount of liquid required in a recipe to get the batter to the right consistency may change from time to time. You may need to adjust the recipe a bit depending on the conditions.

1. Beat the eggs until frothy in a medium bowl. Add the almond flour, butternut squash, coconut flour, and cinnamon. Mix well.

2. Add 2 tablespoons of the almond milk and mix. If the batter seems too thick, add the remaining tablespoon. The desired consistency is not too runny.

3. Heat a nonstick skillet over medium-high heat with enough oil or butter to coat lightly. Spoon the batter onto the griddle, ¼ cup at a time. Cook for about 3–4 minutes, then flip and cook the second side for an additional 2–3 minutes.

4. Remove to serving plate and keep warm until all the pancakes are cooked. Serve with toppings of your choice.

Chestnut Flour Crepes with Raspberry Sauce

These make a lovely brunch offering. Make the crepes and the sauce the night before for easy morning assembly.

INGREDIENTS | YIELDS 12

12 Chestnut Flour Crepes (see recipe in this chapter)
2 pints fresh raspberries, divided
1½ teaspoons lemon juice
¾ cup powdered sugar
2 cups whipped cream

1. Heat the oven to 350°F. Warm the crepes on a baking sheet in the oven for about 5 minutes.

2. Meanwhile, purée 1½ pints raspberries (reserve ½ pint for garnish), lemon juice, and sugar in a blender. Strain through a mesh sieve if you prefer a seedless sauce.

3. Drizzle a tablespoon of the raspberry sauce over each crepe, roll them up, and plate them. Drizzle with more raspberry sauce and garnish with reserved raspberries and whipped cream.

Apple Cinnamon Crepes

Your kids will love these yummy crepes. They're perfect for a special birthday breakfast.

INGREDIENTS | YIELDS 12

10 apples, peeled, cored, and chopped into small cubes
½ packed cup light brown sugar
3 teaspoons ground cinnamon
12 Chestnut Flour Crepes (see recipe in this chapter)
Powdered sugar for garnish

1. Toss the chopped apples with the brown sugar and cinnamon. Let stand for 20 minutes or so.

2. Heat the oven to 350°F and warm the crepes on a baking sheet for about 5 minutes.

3. As soon as you put the crepes in the oven, heat the apples in a skillet on medium-low for 5 minutes.

4. To assemble, spoon the apple-cinnamon mixture onto the open crepes and roll them up. Sprinkle with powdered sugar and serve warm.

Chestnut Flour Crepes

Chestnut flour is sweet and nutty, making the most delicious crepes you can imagine. You can stuff them with fruit and whipped cream or with savory fillings.

INGREDIENTS | YIELDS 12

2 large eggs

1 cup whole milk

½ teaspoon salt

½ cup chestnut flour

½ cup rice flour

2 teaspoons granulated sugar (optional)

1 tablespoon butter (plus more as needed)

Using Nonstick Sauté Pans

Nonstick pans take all of the grief out of making crepes. However, even if your pan is quite new, it's important to use a bit of butter for insurance and extra flavor. Keep the pan well-buttered and you have an almost foolproof method for making perfect crepes.

1. In a food processor, mix the eggs, milk, and salt until blended.

2. With the motor on low, slowly add the flours, stopping occasionally to scrape down the sides of the container.

3. Add the sugar if you are making sweet crepes with sweet filling; omit if you are going to fill them with savory delights.

4. Heat 1 tablespoon butter in a nonstick sauté pan over medium heat. Pour in the batter by a ½ cup. Tilt the pan to spread the batter thinly.

5. Cook the crepes until browned, about 3–4 minutes on each side; place on waxed paper and sprinkle with a bit of rice flour to prevent them from sticking.

6. When the crepes are done, you can fill them right away or store them in the refrigerator or freezer for later use.

Chestnut Crepes with Prosciutto and Peach Sauce

If you can't find mascarpone cheese, use cream cheese. You can make the crepes and sauce and fill the crepes in advance. Just heat everything up at the last moment.

INGREDIENTS | SERVES 4

2 tablespoons cornstarch

¼ cup cold water

2 peaches, blanched, peeled, and sliced

Juice of ½ lemon

1 teaspoon hot red pepper sauce, or to taste

½ cup sugar

½ teaspoon freshly ground black pepper

8 small Chestnut Flour Crepes (see recipe in this chapter)

8 teaspoons mascarpone or cream cheese

8 paper-thin slices of prosciutto ham

1. Mix the cornstarch in cold water until very smooth. Place in a large saucepan with the peaches, lemon juice, hot sauce, and sugar. You may need to add some more water if the peaches are not very juicy. Bring to a boil over medium-high heat, stirring constantly, until very thick and syrupy. Taste for seasonings and add black pepper.

2. Preheat oven to 300°F.

3. Lay the crepes on a large baking sheet and spread with the cheese. Place a slice of ham over each and roll.

4. In a 9" × 9" glass baking pan that has been greased, arrange the rolls, seam-side down, in the pan and bake for 10–15 minutes or until the crepe rolls are hot. Serve hot with the peach syrup.

Mushroom, Ham, and Cheese Crepes

This filling is excellent for brunch, lunch, or a light supper. You can vary the herbs.

INGREDIENTS | YIELDS 12

2 tablespoons olive oil

2 cups cremini mushrooms, brushed clean and chopped

6 sage leaves, shredded

¼ teaspoon salt

¼ teaspoon ground black pepper

½ cup gluten-free ricotta cheese such as Organic Valley

1 large egg, lightly beaten

12 Chestnut Flour Crepes (see recipe in this chapter)

1 recipe Basic Cream Sauce (see recipe in Chapter 11)

½ cup grated Parmesan cheese

1. In a medium sauté pan, add the oil and sauté the mushrooms until softened, 5–7 minutes. Add the sage leaves and salt and pepper. In a bowl, mix the mushrooms with the ricotta and egg.

2. Heat the oven to 350°F. Lay out the crepes. Place 1 tablespoon filling on each. Roll up and place in a baking dish. Cover with Basic Cream Sauce and sprinkle with Parmesan cheese.

3. Bake for 20 minutes. Serve hot.

Corn Crepes with Eggs, Cheese, and Salsa

These Mexican-style crepes make a fantastic brunch!

INGREDIENTS | YIELDS 12

12 Corn Crepes (see recipe in this chapter)

12 thin slices Monterey jack or pepper jack cheese

12 large eggs, poached or fried sunny-side up

12 teaspoons salsa

12 teaspoons grated Parmesan cheese

1. Place the crepes on cookie sheets that have been prepared with nonstick spray. Put a slice of cheese on each crepe. Place 1 egg on each piece of cheese. Spoon 1 teaspoon salsa on top of each egg.

2. Heat the oven to 400°F. Sprinkle the crepes with Parmesan cheese and bake for about 5 minutes, until the cheese is hot and starting to melt.

3. You can put the jack cheese on top of the eggs if you wish and serve the salsa on the side instead.

Corn Crepes

As with the Chestnut Flour Crepes (see this chapter for recipe), you can make these in advance and store them in the refrigerator or freezer.

INGREDIENTS | YIELDS 12

2 large eggs
1 cup whole milk
1 teaspoon salt
1 cup corn flour
2 teaspoons granulated sugar (optional)
2 tablespoons melted butter
Extra butter for frying crepes
(1 tablespoon per crepe)

Storing Crepes

To store crepes, simply put a bit of corn flour on sheets of waxed paper and stack the crepes individually. Then put the whole thing in a plastic bag and store.

1. Place the eggs, milk, and salt in your food processor and mix until smooth. With the motor on low, slowly add the flour and spoon in the sugar if you are making sweet crepes. Scrape down the sides of the bowl often. Add the melted butter.

2. Heat a nonstick sauté pan over medium heat and add 1 tablespoon butter. Pour in ¼ cup of the batter to make one crepe. Tilt the pan to spread the batter evenly.

3. Place the crepes on sheets of waxed paper that have been dusted with extra corn flour.

4. To store, place in a plastic bag in refrigerator or freezer. You can stuff these with salsa, jack cheese, and sour cream, or you can stuff them with mashed fruit such as strawberries.

Mini Strawberry Buckwheat Shortcakes
with Strawberry Coconut Cream

Submitted by Noelle Kelly, SingersKitchen.com. These are quick, healthy, and delicious. The beauty of this recipe is that they can be consumed for breakfast or for dessert.

INGREDIENTS | YIELDS 10 PANCAKES

½ cup buckwheat flour

½ cup gluten-free all-purpose flour

¼ teaspoon salt

¼ teaspoon baking soda

½ tablespoon baking powder

3 tablespoons sugar

2 tablespoons coconut oil

½ cup buttermilk

1 cup light coconut milk

1½ cups sliced fresh strawberries

¼ cup agave nectar

1 teaspoon vanilla extract

½ cup sliced almonds

1. In a medium bowl, mix together the flours, salt, baking soda, baking powder, and sugar. With a fork or pastry blender, cut the coconut oil into the flour. Add the buttermilk and mix well to form a dough.

2. Spoon dough onto a greased cookie sheet, about 2 tablespoons each, for a total of 10 biscuits. Bake for 10 minutes.

3. Blend the coconut milk with the strawberries, agave nectar, and vanilla in a blender to make the strawberry coconut cream sauce.

4. When the shortcakes are cooled, split them in half and spoon the strawberry coconut cream over the bottoms. Sprinkle with almonds and place the shortcake caps on top. Drizzle with more strawberry cream.

Corn Crepes with Salmon and Cream Cheese

Love the taste of smoked salmon and cream cheese? These crepes will hit the spot.
You can substitute unsweetened whipped cream for the cream cheese.

INGREDIENTS | YIELDS 12

12 Corn Crepes (see recipe in this chapter)

4 ounces cream cheese, room temperature

4 ounces sliced smoked salmon

½ sweet onion, sliced thin

Condiments such as horseradish, chopped chives, or mustard

1. Heat the oven to 350°F. Warm the crepes on a baking sheet in the oven for about 5 minutes. Spread with the cream cheese.

2. Place the sliced salmon over the cheese and add the onion slices and condiments if desired.

Bacon, Egg, and Cheese Crepes

Nothing says breakfast like bacon and eggs. Add some cheese,
throw it on a crepe, and you have a gourmet brunch!

INGREDIENTS | YIELDS 6

6 Corn Crepes (see recipe in this chapter)

4 slices bacon, diced

6 large eggs, lightly beaten

½ teaspoon salt

½ cup shredded Cheddar cheese

1. Heat the oven to 350°F. Warm the crepes on a baking sheet in the oven for about 5 minutes.

2. Place the diced bacon in a frying pan and sauté over medium-high heat until browned and crispy.

3. Reduce heat to medium-low. Add the eggs and salt to the pan and stir slowly until cooked through, about 4–5 minutes. Add the cheese, stir to melt, and remove from the heat.

4. Spoon the bacon, egg, and cheese mixture onto the crepes. Roll up and serve hot.

CHAPTER 9

Waffles and French Toast

Cinnamon Banana Belgian Waffles

The combination of cinnamon and banana is absolutely delightful and makes the house smell wonderful. These are a bit labor intensive so you'll probably want to save them for a special occasion. They'd be perfect for a company breakfast.

INGREDIENTS | YIELDS 5

4 large eggs, separated
2 cups whole milk
½ cup ripe mashed banana
2 packed tablespoons light brown sugar
1 teaspoon vanilla extract
1 cup brown rice flour
½ cup sorghum
¾ cup tapioca flour
1 teaspoon xantham gum
2 teaspoons baking powder
¾ teaspoon ground cinnamon
¼ teaspoon ground nutmeg
½ teaspoon salt

Grease Me!

Grease your Belgian waffle maker thoroughly with butter or oil; use a pastry brush to get in the crevices. Because of the bananas in the batter, be sure to cook the waffles an extra minute more than usual. If they stick to the waffle maker, add another ¼ cup tapioca flour to the batter.

1. Preheat a Belgian waffle iron and grease thoroughly with butter or oil.

2. In a medium bowl, whisk together the egg yolks, milk, banana, brown sugar, and vanilla extract.

3. In a large bowl, combine the flours, xanthan gum, baking powder, cinnamon, nutmeg, and salt.

4. Add the liquid ingredients to the dry ingredients and stir until just mixed.

5. In a separate bowl, beat the egg whites until soft peaks form; carefully fold them into the batter.

6. Cook the waffles for about 3–4 minutes or until the waffle maker sensor indicates that it's done and steam no longer escapes.

7. Serve with butter, sliced bananas, and real maple syrup.

Carrot Cake Waffles

Submitted by Rebecca Pytel, Strength and Sunshine. These delectable waffles taste like dessert, but they are nutritious enough to enjoy for breakfast!

INGREDIENTS | YIELDS 2

⅓ cup gluten-free all-purpose flour

¼ teaspoon baking powder

⅛ teaspoon ground ginger

⅛ teaspoon ground nutmeg

¼ teaspoon ground cinnamon

¼ cup sweet carrot purée (use a blender or food processor)

¼ teaspoon pure vanilla extract

⅓ cup water

Vanilla Frosting

Blend 1 tablespoon powdered sugar with enough milk or water to create a runny frosting consistency. Drizzle over the cooked waffles for a decadent treat!

1. Lightly oil and preheat a waffle maker.

2. In a medium bowl, combine all the dry ingredients and whisk together with a fork.

3. Add the wet ingredients; stir to combine until there are no clumps.

4. Pour half the batter into the waffle maker and cook for about 3–4 minutes or until the waffle maker sensor indicates that it's done and steam no longer escapes.

Overnight Oatmeal Waffles

Submitted by Michele Reneau, RealFoodRealtor.com. This recipe is packed with protein and healthy fats and won't leave you hungry like typical waffles. If you don't have a waffle iron, you can use this recipe to make pancakes.

INGREDIENTS | YIELDS 3–4

1 cup gluten-free old-fashioned rolled oats

1 cup cultured buttermilk

⅛ cup coconut flour, sifted

1 tablespoon granulated sugar

½ teaspoon baking powder

½ teaspoon baking soda

¼ teaspoon salt

2 large eggs

¼ cup unsalted butter or coconut oil, melted and cooled

Double Duty

You can easily double this recipe. Store extra waffles in the freezer and reheat in the oven at 350°F for 5–7 minutes.

1. In a large bowl, stir together the oats and cultured buttermilk; cover and set out overnight on the countertop.

2. The next morning, preheat a waffle maker and lightly oil with butter or coconut oil.

3. In a medium bowl, whisk together the flour, sugar, baking powder, baking soda, and salt.

4. In a separate bowl, whisk together the eggs and melted butter. Add the flour mixture; stir until just blended. The batter will be very thick.

5. Heat waffle maker and lightly oil with butter or coconut oil.

6. Cook the waffles on medium-high for 4–5 minutes, about a minute longer than the timer indicates, and steam no longer escapes.

7. Add your favorite toppings and enjoy!

Nutella Waffles with Strawberries

These decadent waffles flavored with Nutella are perfect for a romantic breakfast or a fun dessert.

INGREDIENTS | YIELDS 4

1½ cups gluten-free all-purpose flour (such as Bob's Red Mill)

2 teaspoons baking powder

½ teaspoon baking soda

½ teaspoon salt

2 large eggs

¾ cup whole milk

1 teaspoon vanilla extract

⅓ cup Nutella (or other hazelnut spread)

Sliced strawberries, chocolate sauce, and whipped cream for garnish

How to Tell When Your Waffle Is Done

Most modern-day waffle irons come with a sensor that beeps when the waffle is done. Resist the urge to lift the lid and check on it while it's cooking. Five minutes is a good rule of thumb, but you'll know the waffle is done when steam no longer escapes from the waffle iron. When you lift the lid, the waffle should be lightly browned and crispy.

1. Preheat a waffle maker according to directions and lightly coat with coconut oil or butter.

2. In a medium bowl, mix together the flour, baking powder, baking soda, and salt. Set aside.

3. In a separate bowl, whisk together the eggs, milk, vanilla, and Nutella; add to dry the ingredients and stir to combine.

4. Spoon the batter into the waffle maker; cook for about 3–4 minutes or until the waffle maker sensor indicates that it's done and steam no longer escapes.

5. Top with strawberry slices, chocolate sauce, and whipped cream.

French Toast Soufflé

This recipe comes from Barb Webb, RuralMom.com.

INGREDIENTS | SERVES 10–12

8 ounces cream cheese, softened

8 large eggs

1 bag Udi's Gluten Free Whole Grain Bread

1½ cups milk

½ cup 100% maple syrup

½ cup half-and-half

½ teaspoon vanilla extract

1. Lightly grease a 9" × 13" baking pan.

2. In a medium bowl, beat the cream cheese until smooth with a whisk or mixer. Add the eggs one at a time, mixing until smooth after each add. Beat in milk, half-and-half, maple syrup, and vanilla. Mix ingredients until completely smooth. Set aside.

3. Cut the bread slices into approximately 1" cubes until the entire loaf is cubed. Add the cubed bread to the baking dish, spreading it out in an even layer across the baking dish. Pour the cream cheese mixture over the top of the bread, evenly covering the bread. Cover the baking pan and refrigerate overnight (or for a minimum of 8 hours).

4. When ready to bake, remove the bread mixture from the refrigerator and uncover. Preheat oven to 375°F.

5. Bake for 45–50 minutes. Remove and allow to cool for 10 minutes.

Belgian Pumpkin Waffles

Serve these delicious waffles with maple syrup and whipped cream for a festive fall brunch.

INGREDIENTS | YIELDS 4

¼ packed cup light brown sugar

1½ cups gluten-free all-purpose flour

½ teaspoon xanthan gum

1½ teaspoons baking powder

½ teaspoon salt

2 teaspoons ground cinnamon

1 teaspoon ground ginger

¼ teaspoon ground cloves

¼ teaspoon freshly grated nutmeg

2 large eggs

1 cup whole milk

1 cup canned pumpkin

¼ cup butter, melted

1. Preheat a waffle maker and lightly coat with coconut oil or butter.

2. In a medium bowl, combine the dry ingredients and set aside.

3. Separate the egg yolks from the egg whites. Whip the egg whites with a mixer on high until stiff peaks form. Set aside. Whisk together the egg yolks, milk, pumpkin, and butter. Add the pumpkin mixture to the dry ingredients and stir to combine. Fold in the egg whites.

4. Cook the waffles for about 3–4 minutes or until the waffle maker sensor indicates that it's done and steam no longer escapes..

Baked Pumpkin French Toast

This make-ahead French toast dish brings all the flavors of autumn into your breakfast kitchen!

INGREDIENTS | YIELDS 10–12

4 cups day-old gluten-free bread cubes (such as Udi's)

8 large eggs

2 cups whole milk

1 teaspoon pure vanilla extract

½ cup pumpkin purée

½ teaspoon pumpkin pie spice

¼ packed cup light brown sugar

¼ cup chopped walnuts

1. Place the bread cubes in a greased 9" × 13" baking dish.

2. In a large bowl, whisk together the eggs, milk, vanilla, pumpkin purée, and pumpkin pie spice until combined. Pour over the bread, cover, and refrigerate overnight.

3. Heat the oven to 350°F and bring the casserole to room temperature. Sprinkle with the brown sugar and chopped walnuts. Bake for 35–45 minutes or until set in the middle and golden brown on top. Serve with maple syrup.

Apple Cinnamon French Toast Rollups

This fun twist on French Toast will delight kids and adults alike! This recipe works best with bread that is soft, and the larger the slice, the better. Try Schar or Canyon Bakehouse.

INGREDIENTS | YIELDS 8

8 slices gluten-free white sandwich bread
⅔ cup apple pie filling
2 large eggs
3 tablespoons whole milk
2 teaspoons ground cinnamon
½ cup granulated sugar
3 tablespoons butter
Powdered sugar for garnish

1. Cut the crusts from the bread slices and flatten the slices with a rolling pin.

2. Place the apple pie filling in a small bowl, and use a knife and fork to chop the apples into small pieces.

3. In a shallow dish, whisk together the eggs and milk. In a bowl, mix the cinnamon and sugar.

4. Assemble the French toast rollups by placing a heaping tablespoon of the apple pie filling on ⅓ of each slice of bread. Roll tightly.

5. Heat the butter in a large skillet over medium heat. Dip each roll into the egg mixture and then place in the skillet. Cook in batches, turning occasionally until each roll is lightly browned, about 3–4 minutes. Remove it from the pan and dip immediately in the cinnamon sugar mixture, rolling around to coat. Serve immediately with a sprinkle of powdered sugar.

Baked Cinnamon Raisin Cashew French Toast with Honey Almond Custard

Submitted by Lindsay Cotter, CotterCrunch.com. The cashews and almond butter add healthy proteins to this typically sweet dish.

INGREDIENTS | SERVES 2

1 large egg

1 tablespoon honey

½ cup whole milk

4 slices day-old gluten-free white sandwich bread such Udi's Gluten Free Bread

¼ cup cashews, plain or honey roasted

¼ teaspoon ground cinnamon

1 tablespoon almond butter

Fresh fruit for garnish

1. Preheat oven to 375°F. Lightly oil a 9" × 9" baking dish and set aside.

2. In a medium bowl, combine the egg, honey, and milk. Whisk together.

3. Coat each piece of bread in the egg batter and place in the baking dish. Spread the cashews on top and sprinkle with cinnamon. Bake for 15 minutes, then flip the bread slices and broil for another 1–2 minutes. Be careful you don't burn the cashews.

4. While the French toast is baking, place the leftover egg batter in the microwave and heat for 15–30 seconds to make a custard. Add the almond butter and stir until smooth.

5. Once the bread is baked, top with almond butter topping and fresh fruit. Drizzle with syrup or honey if desired.

Banana and Nutella Stuffed French Toast

You can't go wrong with banana and Nutella. Combine it with French toast and you have a breakfast made in heaven!

INGREDIENTS | YIELDS 4

¾ cup heavy cream

4 large eggs, lightly beaten

½ teaspoon pure vanilla extract

2 teaspoons ground cinnamon

1 tablespoon granulated sugar

8 slices gluten-free white sandwich bread such as Udi's Gluten Free Bread

6 tablespoons Nutella (or other hazelnut spread), divided

2 bananas, thinly sliced

2 tablespoons butter

Maple syrup for topping

1. Combine the cream, eggs, vanilla, cinnamon, and sugar in a shallow dish and set aside.

2. Spread each of 4 bread slices with 1½ tablespoons Nutella. Arrange banana slices over each Nutella-topped bread slice. Top sandwiches with remaining 4 bread slices.

3. Heat the butter in a large frying pan over medium-high heat. Place the sandwiches one at a time into the milk mixture, turn gently to coat both sides, and place in the pan. Cook on each side until lightly browned, 3–4 minutes per side. Garnish with banana slices and maple syrup.

Orange Sour Cream French Toast

This is French toast with the refreshing tang of citrus.

INGREDIENTS | SERVES 6

6 large eggs

½ cup sour cream

½ cup whole milk

½ teaspoon orange zest

1 tablespoon granulated sugar

1 teaspoon pure vanilla extract

½ teaspoon salt

1 loaf day-old gluten-free white sandwich bread such as Udi's Gluten Free Bread

2 tablespoons butter

Orange slices, powdered sugar, and/or maple syrup for toppings

1. In a shallow baking dish or pie plate, whisk together the eggs, sour cream, milk, orange zest, sugar, vanilla, and salt. Place a few slices of the bread in the mixture, turn over, and allow to soak in the liquid for 2–3 minutes.

2. Heat butter in a skillet over medium-high heat. Working in batches, place each piece of soaked bread in the skillet and cook on each side until golden brown, about 2–3 minutes per side. Keep warm in a 200°F oven until ready to serve.

3. Garnish with powdered sugar and orange slices and a drizzle of maple syrup.

French Toast with Fruit Compote

Submitted by Lara Franklin, BetterInBulk.net. You can substitute any of your favorite fruits to make this decadent fruit compote as a topping to your everyday French toast.

INGREDIENTS | SERVES 4–6

6 large eggs

½ cup whole milk

⅛ teaspoon ground cinnamon

1 loaf day-old gluten-free white sandwich bread such as Udi's Gluten Free Bread

3 tablespoons butter, divided

2 cups berries or fruit, cut in bite-size pieces

⅓ cup granulated sugar

1 tablespoon lemon juice

1 teaspoon ground cinnamon

1. In a shallow baking dish or pie plate, whisk together the eggs, milk, and cinnamon. Place a few slices of the bread in the mixture, turn, and soak in the liquid for 2–3 minutes.

2. Heat 2 tablespoons butter in a skillet over medium-high heat. Working in batches, place each piece of soaked bread in the skillet and cook on each side until golden brown, about 3 minutes per side. Keep warm in a 200° oven until ready to serve.

3. Add the remaining butter to a small pan over medium-low heat. Add the remaining ingredients and cook until the mixture thickens and becomes syrupy, 3–5 minutes. Serve over French toast.

Pumpkin Spice French Toast

Submitted by Noelle Kelly, SingersKitchen.com. For those who are vegan, this is the French toast recipe for you! It uses pumpkin spice coconut milk to create this decadent autumn flavor.

INGREDIENTS | SERVES 6

1½ cups pumpkin spice coconut milk (such as So Delicious)

2 small ripe bananas

½ teaspoon vanilla extract

1 tablespoon flaxseed meal

¼ cup pumpkin purée

½ teaspoon ground cinnamon

½ teaspoon pumpkin pie spice (optional)

1 tablespoon maple syrup

1 tablespoon butter

12 slices gluten-free sandwich bread such as Udi's Gluten Free Bread

1. In a pie plate or shallow dish, blend the coconut milk, bananas, vanilla, flaxseed meal, pumpkin purée, cinnamon, pumpkin pie spice (if using), and maple syrup.

2. Heat a griddle to 350°F and melt the butter.

3. Dip each slice of bread in the milk mixture and allow each slice to soak up a bit of the liquid. Add each slice to the griddle and cook for 3–5 minutes on each side or until golden brown. Serve with crushed walnuts or pecans and a little maple syrup and a cup of pumpkin spice coffee.

Baked Eggnog French Toast

Submitted by Astacia Carter, Mamikaze.com. Eggnog makes this recipe a snap! Even better, you can bake it so it's all ready at the same time.

INGREDIENTS | SERVES 6

6 large eggs

⅛ teaspoon salt

1 cup eggnog

2 teaspoons ground cinnamon

1 tablespoon simple syrup

1 loaf stale gluten-free bread (such as Udi's)

Simple Syrup

If you don't have simple syrup, warm 1 tablespoon water in the microwave for 1 minute and add 1 tablespoon granulated sugar. Stir until dissolved.

1. Preheat oven to 450°F with a baking sheet in the oven.

2. Whisk the eggs with the salt. Mix in the eggnog, cinnamon, and simple syrup. Cover and set aside while the oven warms.

3. When the oven is preheated, remove the baking sheet and spray with cooking spray.

4. Soak the bread slices in the egg mixture on each side and place them on the baking sheet. Bake for about 5 minutes. You'll know the slices are ready to flip when the bread has risen slightly and it lifts from the pan easily. Flip and bake for 5 more minutes. Serve warm with butter and maple syrup.

CHAPTER 10

Grains and Cereals

Classic Granola

This basic granola recipe can be the basis for all sorts of variations.
Try adding or substituting your favorite fruits and nuts.

INGREDIENTS | YIELDS 8 CUPS

½ cup honey

½ cup melted coconut oil

⅓ cup water

1 teaspoon vanilla extract

2 cups gluten-free old fashioned rolled oats, such as Bob's Red Mill

½ cup ground flaxseed meal

½ cup unsweetened shredded coconut

1 teaspoon ground cinnamon

½ cup sesame seeds

1 cup sunflower seeds

1 cup chopped nuts of choice

1. Preheat oven to 300°F. In a saucepan over low heat, gently melt the honey with the coconut oil and water. Remove from the heat and add the vanilla.

2. Meanwhile, in a large mixing bowl, mix together the dry ingredients.

3. Add the wet ingredients to the mixing bowl and blend thoroughly.

4. Spread the granola onto a large half-size sheet pan. Toast in oven for 40–50 minutes. Gently stir after every 10 minutes, then more frequently until browned. Let cool completely. Store in an airtight container. Serve with milk or over your favorite yogurt.

Pumpkin Spice Granola

Submitted by Rebecca Pytel, Strength and Sunshine (strengthandsunshine.wordpress.com).
This granola is perfect for fall and winter with the delicious flavors and aromas
of pumpkin, cinnamon, pumpkin pie spice, coconut, and almonds.

INGREDIENTS | YIELDS 2½ CUPS

1½ cups gluten-free old fashioned rolled oats, such as Bob's Red Mill

1 cup crispy brown rice cereal

½ cup slivered almonds

¼ cup unsweetened shredded coconut

2 teaspoons ground cinnamon

1 teaspoon pumpkin pie spice

1 tablespoon granulated sugar

½ cup pumpkin purée

1 tablespoon pure vanilla extract

1. Preheat oven to 325°F. Line a baking sheet with foil and lightly grease with butter or coconut oil.

2. Combine all dry ingredients in a large mixing bowl and stir.

3. In a separate bowl, combine the pumpkin and vanilla. Pour into the dry mix and stir to combine.

4. Spread in a thin layer on the prepared baking sheet. Place the pan in the oven for 30 minutes, stirring every 10 minutes. If you want it extra crunchy, leave it in a bit longer, but be careful not to let it burn.

5. Remove, let cool, and store in an airtight container.

Almond Joy Baked Oatmeal

Submitted by Melissa Angert, girlymama.com. This oatmeal baked in muffin cups is super easy to put together and freezes really well, so you can make a bunch and have them ready when you need them.

INGREDIENTS | YIELDS 12

1 large egg

½ teaspoon vanilla extract

1 cup unsweetened applesauce

¼ cup honey

½ banana, mashed

1½ cups gluten-free old fashioned rolled oats, such as Bob's Red Mill

¼ cup flaxseed meal

1 teaspoon ground cinnamon

1½ teaspoons baking powder

1⅓ cups whole milk

¼ cup shredded coconut

¼ cup sliced almonds

¼ cup dark chocolate chips

1. Preheat oven to 350°F. Line a 12-cup muffin tin with liners.

2. In a large bowl, combine the egg, vanilla, applesauce, honey, and banana. Mix in the oats, flax meal, cinnamon, and baking powder. Slowly mix in the milk. (It will be a little runny.) Fold in the coconut, almonds, and chocolate chips.

3. Scoop about ¼ cup of oatmeal into each muffin cup in the prepared tin. Bake for about 30 minutes or until a toothpick inserted in the center comes out clean. Freeze leftovers for up to 4 weeks. Before eating, reheat in the microwave for 20–30 seconds.

Berry Banana Baked Oatmeal

Submitted by Trina O'Boyle, OboyOrganic.com. As this dish bakes in the oven, the smell fills the house with the amazing smell of fruit and sugar, and the warmth of the oatmeal fills your belly!

INGREDIENTS | SERVES 6

3 tablespoons melted butter

2 cups gluten-free old-fashioned rolled oats

1 teaspoon baking powder

1½ teaspoons ground cinnamon

½ teaspoon salt

⅓ packed cup light brown sugar

½ cup crushed almonds, pecans, and walnuts

2 teaspoons pure vanilla extract

1 large egg

2 cups whole milk

2 bananas

2 cups mixed berries, frozen or fresh

1. Preheat oven to 375°F. Grease a 9" × 11" baking pan. Melt the butter in a small saucepan and set aside.

2. In a large mixing bowl, combine the oats, baking powder, cinnamon, salt, brown sugar, and nuts. In a smaller bowl, combine the vanilla, egg, and milk.

3. Slice the bananas and place them on the bottom of the prepared pan. Add half the berries and pour the oat mixture on top. Add the milk-egg mixture on top of the oats. Add the remaining berries and drizzle with the melted butter. Bake for 30–40 minutes.

Almond Quinoa Hot Cereal

Submitted by Noelle Kelly, SingersKitchen.com. This cereal is packed with protein and is incredibly filling.

INGREDIENTS | SERVES 3

1 cup quinoa, rinsed and drained

1 cup almond milk (or milk of choice)

1 cup water

1 teaspoon ground cinnamon

1 teaspoon vanilla extract

1 banana, sliced

½ cup sliced almonds

3 tablespoons fig butter (optional)

3 tablespoons coconut sugar (optional)

1. Add the quinoa to a small pot and cover with the almond milk and water. Stir in the cinnamon and vanilla.

2. Cook over medium-low heat for 25 minutes or until the quinoa has absorbed the liquid. Once it is cooked, add the banana, almonds and fig butter (if using). Sprinkle with coconut sugar if you like it sweeter. Serve warm.

Bacon and Cheese Oatmeal

Submitted by JessieLeigh Smith, ParentingMiracles.net. Not all oatmeal needs to be sweet. This rich and savory recipe is tasty and will stick to your ribs.

INGREDIENTS | SERVES 6–8

2 cups gluten-free old-fashioned rolled oats

4 cups water

8 strips bacon, cooked and crumbled (reserve bacon grease)

4 ounces Cheddar cheese, shredded

1. Bring the oats and water to a boil in a medium saucepan. Reduce heat and simmer until cooked, about 5 minutes.

2. Stir in 2 tablespoons of the reserved bacon grease. Mix in the bacon and Cheddar. Stir until the cheese is melted throughout.

3. Dish into cereal bowls and serve immediately.

Blueberry Breakfast Quinoa

*Usually served as a dinnertime side dish, quinoa makes a
wonderful hot cereal and it's packed with protein.*

INGREDIENTS | SERVES 3–4

2 cups whole milk

1 cup quinoa, rinsed and drained

¼ cup light brown sugar

½ teaspoon ground cinnamon

½ teaspoon vanilla extract

1 cup fresh blueberries

Heavy whipping cream and brown sugar
for topping

1. Bring the milk and quinoa to a boil in a medium saucepan. Reduce heat to low, cover, and cook for 15 minutes.

2. Stir in the brown sugar and cinnamon. Cook for another 5–8 minutes or until the milk is absorbed. Stir in the vanilla and blueberries. Dish into cereal bowls, drizzle with cream, and sprinkle with brown sugar.

Peppermint Chocolate Quinoa Flakes

*Submitted by Rebecca Pytel, Strength and Sunshine. Real peppermint tea and pure peppermint
extract in this breakfast porridge gives you that clean, fresh feeling, like a breath of fresh air.*

INGREDIENTS | SERVES 1

⅓ cup quinoa flakes

1 tablespoon chocolate protein powder

1½ tablespoons unsweetened
cocoa powder

8 ounces hot brewed peppermint tea
(use 1 tea bag)

¼ teaspoon pure peppermint extract

1. Place all the dry ingredients into a microwave-safe bowl and stir.

2. Add the tea to the bowl along with the peppermint extract and stir. Microwave on high for 2 minutes. Serve hot.

Baked Soaked Oatmeal

Submitted by Kelly Moeggenborg, KellytheKitchenKop.com. Baked soaked oatmeal is a nutritious and simple healthy breakfast recipe.

INGREDIENTS | SERVES 12

2½ cups gluten-free old-fashioned rolled oats

1¾ cups buttermilk

½ cup coconut oil, melted and cooled

4 large eggs

½ cup maple syrup

1 teaspoon baking powder

½ teaspoon salt

2 teaspoons ground cinnamon

2 teaspoons pure vanilla extract

1 cup raisins (optional)

2 cups chopped apples or pears (optional)

Why Soaked Oats?

Oats contain phytic acid, which can be hard on the digestive system. Soaking the oats overnight in an acid medium helps break down the phytic acid, thus making the oatmeal easier to digest.

1. Combine the oats and buttermilk in a glass mixing bowl and cover. Let stand on the counter for 12–24 hours.

2. In the morning, preheat the oven to 350°F. Grease a 9" × 13" baking dish.

3. In a large bowl, combine the oil, eggs, and syrup and beat until glossy. Mix in the baking powder, salt, cinnamon, and vanilla.

4. Fold in the soaked oats along with the raisins and chopped apples or pears, if using. Pour into the prepared baking dish and bake for 25–30 minutes or until lightly browned on top. Serve with a sprinkling of brown sugar.

Slow Cooker Groats

Submitted by Trina O'Boyle, OboyOrganic.com. Oat Groats are oats that have been hulled but left whole, thus retaining their high nutritional value because they haven't been extensively processed. They take a long time to cook, making them perfect for the slow cooker!

INGREDIENTS | SERVES 4

2 cups gluten-free oat groats

6 cups water

2 cinnamon sticks

1 teaspoon salt

½ packed cup light brown sugar

½ cup dried fruit, optional

Fresh or dried fruit, maple syrup, brown sugar, milk for topping.

Add all the ingredients except the toppings to a 4- or 6-quart slow cooker and cook on low for 8–10 hours. Serve with your choice of toppings.

Hazelnut Coffee Oat Bake

Submitted by Rebecca Pytel, Strength and Sunshine (strengthandsunshine.wordpress.com). This yummy twist on traditional oatmeal highlights the flavors of hazelnut and coffee to create a delicious treat.

INGREDIENTS | SERVES 1

⅓ cup gluten-free old-fashioned rolled oats

⅓ cup water

½ teaspoon hazelnut extract

¼ teaspoon baking powder

2 tablespoons unsweetened cocoa powder

1 teaspoon instant coffee

10 raw hazelnuts

1. Preheat oven to 350°F. Grease a single-serve ramekin.

2. Combine all the ingredients except the nuts in a small bowl and mix. Pour the mixture into the prepared ramekin and bake for 20 minutes, covered with foil. Uncover and bake for another 4 minutes. Top with hazelnuts and serve.

Quinoa Oatmeal

Submitted by Trina O'Boyle, OboyOrganic.com. Mixing quinoa into your oatmeal is a great way to ramp up the protein and fiber without giving up the taste and texture of the oats.

INGREDIENTS | SERVES 4

1 cup gluten-free old-fashioned rolled oats

1 cup quinoa, rinsed and drained

3 cups water

Toppings: brown sugar, honey, fruit, or yogurt

Place the oats and quinoa in a medium pot with the water. You can let it soak overnight if you wish. Heat to medium-high and let the mixture begin to boil, then reduce heat to low and simmer for about 15 minutes, until fluffy and the liquid is absorbed. Top with fruit, brown sugar, honey, yogurt, or just eat it plain.

Hot Ground Flax Cereal Bowl

This recipes comes from Elle, a blogger at WeCanBegintoFeed.blogspot.com. This grain-free cereal is high in protein, filling, and quite delightful.

INGREDIENTS | SERVES 2

1 banana, peeled and mashed

1 scoop protein powder

½ cup egg whites

2 tablespoons ground flaxseeds

1 teaspoon ground cinnamon

¼ cup unsweetened vanilla almond milk

1. In a large bowl, mash the banana; add the rest of the ingredients and stir until combined.

2. Pour the mixture into a small saucepan over medium heat. Stir until the mixture thickens and doubles in volume, about 7–8 minutes.

3. Divide between 2 bowls and top with your favorite topping such as yogurt, berries, or fruit.

Pumpkin Oat Bars

Submitted by Lindsay Cotter, CotterCrunch.com. These breakfast bars are super nutritious and easy to make. They are the perfect for an on-the-go fall breakfast or mid-afternoon snack with a cup of tea.

INGREDIENTS | SERVES 4

1 cup pumpkin purée

¼ cup coconut milk or milk of choice

2 tablespoons old-fashioned unsulphured molasses (optional)

1 large egg

1 teaspoon baking soda

Dash of salt

2 teaspoons ground cinnamon

¼ packed cup light brown sugar

1 cup gluten-free old-fashioned rolled oats

⅓ cup almond flour (coconut flour works too)

1. Preheat oven to 375°F. Grease a 9" × 9" baking pan.

2. In a large bowl, stir to combine the pumpkin purée, milk, molasses, and egg. Add the remaining ingredients and mix until blended.

3. Pour into the prepared baking pan. Bake for 25–30 minutes until set. Cool and cut into bars.

Molasses

Molasses can be used when baking as a sugar alternative. It adds a rich, caramelized flavor to baked goods. Molasses is the dark, sticky syrup left behind after the sugar has been boiled out of cane and beet juices. There are several stages to this process, yielding light, dark, and blackstrap molasses as the syrup is cooked down. Light and dark molasses can be used interchangeably in baking, but steer clear of blackstrap molasses unless you are looking for the nutritional benefits. It is very high in calcium and iron, which is fantastic, but be prepared for its strong flavor.

CHAPTER 11

Sauces and Side Dishes

Fried Green Tomatoes

*Use tomatoes that are very firm. They usually aren't very large, so count on
2 per person. Serve with thick slices of country ham or Canadian bacon.*

INGREDIENTS | SERVES 4

1 cup corn flour

1 teaspoon salt

⅛ teaspoon ground black pepper

1 cup cornmeal

2 large eggs, whisked

8 green tomatoes, cores trimmed, cut into ⅓" slices

Sour cream for topping (optional)

1. In a small bowl, mix the flour, salt, and pepper. Place the cornmeal in another bowl and the whisked eggs in a third bowl.

2. Dip the tomato slices first in the flour, then in the egg, and then coat them with cornmeal.

3. Heat ½" of oil in a frying pan to 350°F. Slide the tomato slices into the pan and fry for 4 minutes or until well browned. Flip the tomatoes and finish frying on the other side, another 3–4 minutes.

4. Drain on paper towels. Serve as a side dish with eggs and bacon. You can also add a dollop of sour cream to each tomato slice.

Classic Hollandaise Sauce

*This classic sauce is wonderful over asparagus, and it's also used for
the Eggs Benedict with Asparagus recipe in Chapter 2.*

INGREDIENTS | YIELDS 2 CUPS

4 egg yolks

1 tablespoon water

1½ tablespoons lemon juice

1 cup soft butter

¼ teaspoon salt

¼ teaspoon ground black pepper

1. Whisk together the egg yolks, water, and lemon juice in a medium saucepan for 2–3 minutes, until thick and pale. Set the pan over medium-low heat and continue to whisk briskly, moving the pan around so the eggs don't cook too fast, as the eggs become thick and frothy.

2. When the eggs become thick enough to see the bottom of the pan as you stir, remove from the heat. Add the soft butter a spoonful at a time, whisking between each addition. Continue whisking until the butter is fully incorporated and the sauce is smooth.

3. Season with salt and pepper. Taste and adjust seasonings if necessary.

Cherry Tomatoes on the Side

This recipe comes from Beth Christian, Burlington County Editor, JerseyBites.com.
Best with fresh cherry tomatoes in season, this dish is a great accompaniment to eggs.

INGREDIENTS | SERVES 6

1 tablespoon olive oil
2 pints cherry tomatoes
¼ teaspoon sea salt
⅛ teaspoon freshly ground black pepper
2 teaspoons chopped fresh thyme leaves
¼ cup freshly grated Parmesan cheese

1. Heat the oil in skillet over medium-high heat. Add the tomatoes to the pan and season with salt and pepper. Sauté for 4–5 minutes, moving the tomatoes around the pan several times.

2. Toss the thyme on top and mix carefully with a spoon. Remove with a slotted spoon, sprinkle with Parmesan, and serve immediately.

Ham and Asparagus Rolls with Cheese

This recipe is a lovely addition to any brunch table, though it's hearty enough to eat on its own.

INGREDIENTS | SERVES 6

1 bunch frozen asparagus
½ pound smoked ham, sliced thin
½ pound white American cheese, sliced thin
1 recipe Creamy Cheddar Sauce with Ham and Sherry (see recipe in this chapter)

1. Preheat oven to 350°F. Butter a 13" × 9" glass baking pan.

2. Drop the frozen asparagus in boiling water for 1 minute and dry on paper towels. Lay out the slices of ham. Place a slice of cheese and then an asparagus spear on each ham slice. Roll up and secure with toothpicks if necessary.

3. Place the rolls in the prepared pan. Pour the cheese sauce over the top. Bake for 25 minutes or until lightly browned on top and heated through. Serve hot.

Creamy Cheddar Sauce with Ham and Sherry

This is excellent over vegetables, spaghetti squash, or rice.

INGREDIENTS | YIELDS 2½ CUPS

3 tablespoons unsalted butter

3 tablespoons corn flour

2 cups milk or heavy cream, warmed

⅔ cup grated sharp Cheddar cheese

¼ cup minced smoked ham

2 teaspoons sherry

¼ teaspoon salt

¼ teaspoon ground black pepper

1. In a medium frying pan, melt the butter and stir in the flour over medium-low heat. Sauté, stirring for 4–5 minutes. Add the warm milk or cream, whisking constantly until thickened to desired consistency.

2. Remove from the heat and stir in the cheese, ham, sherry, and salt and pepper. Serve.

Sherry as a Flavoring

There are several kinds of sherry used in cooking, dry and sweet. Sweet sherry is often called cream sherry, as in Harveys Bristol Cream. Really good sherry is made in Spain by British companies that export it all over the world. The Chinese love it in sauces and soups, and it does add a wonderful flavor. It's also good in shrimp bisque, lobster Newburg, and other seafood dishes.

Crispy Potato Pancakes

This is basically a good old kosher recipe. It is marvelous with applesauce, sour cream, or both. For brunch, it's excellent with eggs on the side.

1. In a large bowl, mix together the grated potatoes, onions, eggs, potato flour, salt, and pepper.

2. Heat ½" olive oil in a skillet over medium heat and spoon in the potato cakes, pressing down to make patties.

3. Fry until golden brown, about 5 minutes per side. Drain, keep warm, and serve with garnish of choice.

The Origins of Potato Pancakes

During the long winters in northern and eastern Europe, when fresh fruits and vegetables were not available, winter storage of carrots, potatoes, beets, Brussels sprouts, apples, and dried fruits was crucial to prevent scurvy, or ascorbic acid deficiency. As nature would have it, these vegetables are packed with vitamins and minerals. Potato pancakes with sour cream, applesauce, or fruit syrups became a staple in harsh climates.

Scalloped Potatoes with Leeks and Country Ham

This is a great brunch or supper dish. It's filling and delicious, and especially good on a cold day or nippy evening.

INGREDIENTS | SERVES 6

1½ cups grated Parmesan cheese

1 cup coarsely grated Fontina cheese

½ cup corn flour

¼ teaspoon salt

¼ teaspoon ground black pepper

6 Idaho or Yukon gold potatoes, peeled and sliced thinly

4 leeks, thinly sliced crosswise (white parts only)

1 pound deli ham, diced

3 cups whole milk

4 tablespoons butter, divided

1. Preheat oven to 350°F. Butter a 13" × 9" glass baking pan.

2. In a medium bowl, mix together the cheeses, corn flour, salt, and pepper.

3. Place a layer of potatoes in the baking dish, then sprinkle ¼ of the leeks and ¼ of the ham on top. Sprinkle with ¼ of the cheese mixture. Repeat until you get to the top of the baking dish. Add the milk and dot with the butter.

4. Bake for about 90 minutes. The top should be brown and crispy, the inside soft and creamy.

Basic Cream Sauce

This cream sauce is the basis for a lot of cooking. You can use milk instead of cream, but don't substitute margarine for butter.

INGREDIENTS | YIELDS 2 CUPS

3 tablespoons unsalted butter

3 tablespoons corn flour

2 cups whole milk or heavy cream, warmed

¼ teaspoon salt

¼ teaspoon ground black pepper

⅛ teaspoon ground nutmeg, 1 teaspoon Dijon mustard, or 1 tablespoon snipped fresh chives (optional)

1. In a small saucepan over medium-low heat, melt the butter and stir in the flour. Sauté, stirring for 4–5 minutes.

2. Add the warm milk or cream, whisking constantly until thickened to desired consistency.

3. Just before serving, add the salt and pepper. The optional ingredients can be added at this time.

Beyond the Basics

Once you learn to make a basic cream sauce, you can add mustard, sautéed mushrooms, oysters, shrimp, herbs, and all kinds of luscious things. You can pour the sauce over fish or shellfish, poultry, and/or vegetables.

Parmesan-Crusted Asparagus

Use fresh asparagus for best results.

INGREDIENTS | SERVES 8

2 cups grated Parmesan cheese, divided

1 cup gluten-free Italian seasoned bread crumbs

2 tablespoons butter, melted

½ teaspoon salt

¼ teaspoon ground black pepper

3 egg whites (from large eggs)

1 tablespoon granulated sugar

2 pounds thick asparagus spears, washed and trimmed

Homemade Gluten-Free Bread Crumbs

If you can't find the store-bought variety, it is very easy to make bread crumbs at home. Toast 4 slices gluten-free bread, cool, and process in a food processor to make crumbs. For seasoned bread crumbs, add 1 teaspoon each ground thyme, dried basil, dried rosemary, dried oregano, and ½ teaspoon garlic powder. Pulsate a few times to combine.

1. Preheat oven to 450°F. Grease a large, rimmed baking sheet with olive oil.

2. Combine 1½ cups Parmesan, bread crumbs, butter, salt, and pepper in a 9" × 13" baking pan.

3. In a bowl, whip the egg whites and sugar until soft peaks form. Add the asparagus and toss. Dredge each spear in the bread crumb mixture and place on the prepared baking sheet.

4. Bake for 6–8 minutes or until just starting to brown. Sprinkle with the remaining Parmesan cheese and finish baking until the cheese is melted, about 5 minutes. Plate and serve immediately.

Southern Cheese Grits

This recipe has been shared by Melissa Jennings, StockpilingMoms.com.
This dish is the perfect accompaniment to bacon and eggs.

INGREDIENTS | SERVES 10

8 cups water
½ cup butter
2 cups quick-cooking grits
2 large eggs, lightly beaten
4 cups shredded sharp Cheddar cheese
1 teaspoon salt
½ teaspoon ground black pepper
1 tablespoon garlic powder
¼ cup grated Parmesan cheese

What on Earth Is a Grit?

Grits are ground from dried corn kernels that have had the hull and germ removed. (Cornmeal is ground from the dried corn kernels without the hull and germ removed.) Grits can be simmered in water, chicken stock, or milk. Because of their mild flavor, you typically add butter and salt or cheese.

1. Preheat oven to 350°F. Grease a 9" × 13" baking dish with butter.

2. Bring the water to a boil in a large Dutch oven over medium-high heat. Whisk in the butter and grits. Reduce heat to low and simmer while whisking constantly for 5–7 minutes or until the grits are done. They will be about the consistency of cream of wheat.

3. Remove from heat and stir 1 cup of grits into the eggs. Add the egg mixture to the pot. Add the Cheddar cheese, salt, pepper, and garlic powder and stir to combine.

4. Pour the grits into the prepared pan and sprinkle with the Parmesan cheese. Bake covered for 40 minutes or until the mixture is set and starts to turn golden brown. Serve and enjoy!

Italian Ricotta-Chestnut Fritters

*This is a traditional Italian recipe. These fritters are a wonderful
side dish at brunch, and they're simple to make.*

INGREDIENTS | SERVES 4

2 large eggs
½ cup granulated sugar
1 teaspoon baking soda
1 cup gluten-free ricotta cheese such as
Organic Valley
½ cup chestnut flour
½ cup rice flour
Powdered sugar, to dust fritters

1. In a medium bowl, beat together the eggs and sugar until thick.

2. Slowly add the rest of the ingredients except the powdered sugar. Cover the bowl and let stand for 1 hour.

3. Heat 2" of oil over medium-high heat in a deep frying pan. Drop the batter by tablespoons into the oil. Do not overfill the pan. Fry for about 2 minutes, turning as they brown.

4. Drain on brown paper or paper towels and dust with powdered sugar.

Home Fries

*These roasted potatoes are delicious alongside your eggs for breakfast or
mixed with sausage and veggies as part of a breakfast skillet.*

INGREDIENTS | SERVES 6–8

4 Idaho potatoes, washed and diced
1 teaspoon salt
2 tablespoons olive oil
1 teaspoon Lawry's Seasoned Salt

1. Preheat oven to 400°F. Grease a large, rimmed baking sheet with olive oil.

2. Meanwhile, place the diced potatoes in a 3-quart pot of water and bring to a boil over medium-high heat. Boil for exactly 7 minutes. Drain immediately in a colander and shake them around to roughen up the edges.

3. Spread the boiled potatoes out onto the prepared baking sheet and drizzle with the olive oil. Sprinkle with Lawry's Seasoned Salt.

4. Bake for 50–60 minutes or until golden brown and crispy.

Quinoa, Corn, and Bean Salad

This recipes comes from Kelly Dabel, WholesomeDinnerTonight.blogspot .com. This fresh salad is perfect for a summer brunch table.

INGREDIENTS | SERVES 6–8

1 cup quinoa, rinsed and drained

2 cups water

1 (15-ounce) can corn, rinsed and drained

1 (15-ounce) can black beans, rinsed and drained

1 small zucchini, cubed

½ English cucumber, cubed

½ red bell pepper, diced

1 cup cherry tomatoes

¼ cup finely chopped fresh cilantro

½ cup Quinoa Salad Dressing (see sidebar)

¼ teaspoon salt

¼ teaspoon ground black pepper

1. In a medium saucepan, combine the quinoa and water and heat on medium-high. Bring to a boil. Reduce heat to low and simmer for about 15 minutes, until the water is absorbed. Fluff with a fork and set aside.

2. In a large salad bowl, combine the corn, beans, zucchini, cucumber, bell pepper, tomatoes, and cilantro.

3. Once the quinoa is cooled, add it to the vegetables and stir to combine. Add the dressing and stir to coat. Add the salt and pepper and toss. This salad keeps well in the refrigerator for 3–4 days.

Quinoa Salad Dressing

For the dressing, combine ¼ cup fresh-squeezed lemon juice (about 1 lemon), ¼ cup olive oil, ½ teaspoon ground cumin, ¼ teaspoon salt, and ⅛ teaspoon ground black pepper.

Beet and Goat Cheese Salad

Beets are a great source of iron, and the combination of beets and goat cheese is delightful. For a special treat at your next brunch, serve this salad with Sugar-Coated Pecans (see sidebar) on top.

INGREDIENTS | SERVES 6

4 medium beets
½ cup extra-virgin olive oil
Juice of 1 lemon
1 teaspoon granulated sugar
½ teaspoon Dijon mustard
½ teaspoon salt
¼ teaspoon ground black pepper
1 (12-ounce) bag spring mix salad greens
3 ounces goat cheese
Sugar-Coated Pecans (see sidebar), optional

How to Make Sugar-Coated Pecans

Beat 1 egg white with 1 tablespoon water until frothy. In a separate bowl, combine 1 cup granulated sugar with ¾ teaspoon salt and ½ teaspoon ground cinnamon. Toss 1 pound pecan halves first in the egg whites and then in the sugar mixture. Spread them on a baking sheet and cook for 1 hour at 250°F, stirring every 15 minutes. Cool and store in an airtight container for up to 1 week.

1. Cut the greens off the beets, leaving about 1" of the greens intact. Snip the root, leaving about 1" on the beet. Leave the skin on. (If you cut off the top and bottom of the beet and/or peel it, the juices will seep into the cooking water and you'll lose valuable nutrients.) Boil the beets in a medium saucepan over medium-high heat for 30–45 minutes or until fork tender.

2. In a bowl, whisk together the oil, lemon juice, sugar, mustard, salt, and pepper for the salad dressing.

3. When the beets are finished cooking, carefully remove them from the hot water and peel them under cold running water. Allow them to cool slightly and then chop them into a medium dice.

4. For individual servings, place a handful of salad greens on each plate. Drizzle with the dressing and then top with diced beets and crumbled goat cheese. Add Sugar-Coated Pecans if desired.

Cauli-Slaw

Submitted by Cindy Dudas from her blog, What the Heck's a BonBon?
*(http://whateverworks.typepad.com/bonbon). Cauliflower, rather than cabbage,
is the base for this delicious slaw—perfect for a winter brunch table.*

INGREDIENTS | SERVES 6

3 tablespoons gluten-free rice vinegar

1 tablespoon apple cider vinegar

2 teaspoons granulated sugar

⅓ cup mayonnaise

¼ teaspoon salt

¼ teaspoon ground black pepper

½ head cauliflower, sliced very thin

1 small stalk celery, minced

½ cup shredded carrots

⅛ cup red onion, minced

¼ cup yellow bell pepper, minced

1. In a small bowl, whisk together the vinegars, sugar, mayonnaise, salt, and pepper to make the dressing.

2. Place the vegetables in a large bowl, drizzle with dressing, and toss.

Pizza Quinoa Pasta Salad

*This recipe was submitted by Karla Walsh, HealthfulBitesBlog.com. Quinoa is loaded
with protein and is naturally gluten-free. This version of quinoa salad uses herbs and
cheese to achieve a great Italian flavor without a dressing, so it's very low in fat.*

INGREDIENTS | SERVES 2

1 cup water

½ cup quinoa, rinsed and drained

½ cup diced red onion

½ cup diced tomato

1 clove garlic, minced

1 teaspoon dried basil

½ teaspoon paprika

½ teaspoon dried oregano

¼ teaspoon salt

1 ounce mozzarella or Parmesan cheese, shredded

1. Bring the water to a boil in a medium saucepan. Lower heat to a simmer, add the quinoa, and stir. Cover and simmer for about 20 minutes, until all the liquid is absorbed. Remove from heat.

2. Pour the quinoa into a large mixing bowl and add the remaining ingredients. Toss lightly to combine.

Spinach and Strawberry Poppy Seed Salad

Spinach is rich in iron and beta-carotene, and it's a great source of fiber. Strawberries are also a good source of fiber as well as vitamin C and antioxidants. The contrast of red berries against the green spinach makes a beautiful presentation on a holiday brunch table.

INGREDIENTS | SERVES 6

½ cup walnut halves

4 scallions, trimmed and chopped

½ cup granulated sugar

¾ cup raspberry vinegar

1 teaspoon dry mustard

1 teaspoon salt

1 tablespoon Worcestershire sauce

1 cup extra-virgin olive oil

1 teaspoon poppy seeds

9-ounce package fresh baby spinach

1 cup watercress (optional, but a nice addition)

3 cups sliced fresh strawberries

The Vinegar Controversy

Vinegar is quite controversial in the gluten-free community because many vinegars are derived from gluten-free grains. While they generally test well below the less than 20 parts per million gluten threshold that is considered "gluten-free," people who are extremely sensitive may notice a reaction when they consume vinegar. Malt vinegar is a definite no-no. Distilled white vinegar can be made from almost any starch source or a combination, so it's highly controversial; proceed with caution. Apple cider vinegar should be safe as it's derived from apples. With all other vinegars, it is best to contact the manufacturer if you are concerned. Most people won't have a reaction to vinegar, but if you are celiac or very sensitive, it is best to be cautious.

1. Heat the walnut halves in a large dry skillet over medium heat for 3–5 minutes, stirring constantly, until golden brown. Remove the walnuts to a cutting board and allow them to cool. Before adding them to the salad, roughly chop them with a chef's knife.

2. To make the dressing, place the scallions in a blender or food processor along with the sugar, vinegar, mustard, salt, and Worcestershire sauce. Blend or pulse to combine. Then slowly add the olive oil while blending until thoroughly incorporated. Pour the dressing into a jar, add the poppy seeds, and shake.

3. For individual servings, place a handful of baby spinach on each salad plate. Add some watercress on top. Sprinkle with strawberries and chopped toasted walnuts and drizzle with dressing.

Seasoned Black Beans

Seasoned black beans are great to have on hand. They are a great addition to salads and wraps.

INGREDIENTS | SERVES 6

1 pound dried black beans
8 cups water
1 tablespoon olive oil
½ cup chopped white onion
5 cloves garlic, minced
3 teaspoons ground cumin
2 teaspoons dried oregano
½ teaspoon red pepper flakes
¼ cup chopped fresh cilantro
2 teaspoons salt

1. Place the beans in a large bowl with 4 cups of water, cover, and leave on the counter overnight.

2. Heat the oil in a large Dutch oven over medium heat. Add the onions and cook until soft and translucent, about 5 minutes. Add the garlic and cook for another minute. Stir in the cumin, oregano, and pepper flakes. Cook for another minute.

3. Add the beans to the pot along with the remaining 4 cups of water and stir. Bring to a boil, then reduce heat to low and cover. Simmer for 1 hour.

4. Add the cilantro and salt. Cover and cook for an additional 30–60 minutes, until the beans are tender and thick. Taste and adjust seasonings. Serve as a side dish or add to salads or nachos. Also great in breakfast wraps.

Crispy Potato Veggie Cakes

This is another recipe from Cindy Dudas, from her blog, What the Heck's a BonBon? (http://whateverworks.typepad.com/bonbon). These crispy potato pancakes are loaded with vegetables, making them a nutritious breakfast or side dish to a plate of eggs.

INGREDIENTS | SERVES 6

¾ cup gluten-free all-purpose flour

½ teaspoon baking powder

¼ teaspoon salt

⅛ teaspoon garlic powder

1 small yellow onion, grated

2 large eggs

¼ cup shredded carrots

¼ cup frozen sweet corn kernels, thawed

¼ cup chopped kale

¼ cup diced green and/or red bell pepper

¼ cup chopped broccoli

¼ cup shredded zucchini

2 large russet potatoes, peeled and grated

2–3 cups canola oil

Avoid Brown Potatoes

Place the grated potatoes in a bowl of ice water, seasoned with 1 teaspoon salt. Make sure they are fully covered with water. This keeps them from turning brown. Let them sit while you prepare the rest of the recipe.

1. In a small bowl, combine the flour, baking powder, salt, and garlic powder.

2. In a large bowl, combine the onion, eggs, and vegetables (minus the potatoes) and lightly stir them together. Stir in the flour mixture.

3. Drain the potatoes, squeezing out as much water as possible, and stir them into the vegetable mixture.

4. Heat the oil in a large sauté pan over medium heat. Using an ice-cream scoop or a spoon, scoop a small amount of the mixture and very carefully place it in the hot oil. You can press it down slightly with a spatula, or leave it a bit loose to give it a more crispy texture. Add about 4 more cakes to the oil (depending on your pan size), stirring the mixture in the bowl between each scoop so you get a good combination of ingredients in each.

5. Fry the cakes for about 4–5 minutes per side, until both sides are golden brown. Remove from the pan and drain on paper towels. Repeat with remaining batter.

Roasted Brussels Sprouts with Caramelized Onions and Bacon

Roasted Brussels sprouts are delicious in their own right, but add sweetly caramelized onions and crispy bacon and you have a culinary masterpiece. Serve these for your next brunch and watch your guests gobble them up!

INGREDIENTS | SERVES 6

1 pound Brussels sprouts

2 tablespoons olive oil

¼ teaspoon salt

¼ teaspoon ground black pepper

4 slices bacon, diced

1 red onion, sliced

1 tablespoon chopped fresh parsley, optional

1. Preheat oven to 400°F. Trim the ends of the Brussels sprouts, and cut the larger ones in half. Place them in a bowl and drizzle with olive oil. Sprinkle with salt and pepper. Toss until well coated, and then spread out evenly on a large, rimmed sheet pan.

2. In a large skillet over medium-high heat, cook the diced bacon until it is nice and brown, 5–10 minutes. Remove the bacon to paper towels with a slotted spoon to cool. Leave the bacon grease in the pan, add the onions, and reduce the heat to low.

3. Place the pan of Brussels sprouts in the oven and roast for 15–20 minutes or until they are nicely browned, turning once halfway through so they brown evenly.

4. While the Brussels sprouts are roasting, keep stirring the onions every few minutes, allowing them to cook slowly until they are soft, brown, and caramelized, about 20 minutes.

5. Combine the roasted Brussels sprouts, caramelized onions, and crispy bacon bits in a serving bowl. Season with more salt and pepper if desired. Top with chopped parsley if using. Serve immediately.

Bacon-Stuffed Avocados

This recipe is courtesy of Laura Franklin, BetterInBulk.net. These little bacon-stuffed avocado "boats" are satisfying, filling, and delicious. They make a nutritious breakfast, or they can be served as an appetizer.

INGREDIENTS | SERVES 4

4 medium ripe avocados

8 slices bacon, cooked until crisp and crumbled

¼ teaspoon lime juice

½ cup butter

¼ packed cup light brown sugar

¼ cup white wine vinegar

¼ cup chopped garlic

½ teaspoon salt

1. Slice the avocados in half lengthwise; scoop out about half of the avocado flesh from each of the halves, leaving a small "bowl" in each. Place the scooped-out avocado in a medium bowl; add the bacon and mash gently. Spoon the mixture back into each avocado half. Sprinkle with lime juice to prevent browning.

2. Combine the remaining ingredients in a small saucepan; bring to a boil over medium-high heat, stirring occasionally, until smooth and all the sugars are dissolved, 4–5 minutes. Pour the hot mixture over the filled avocado halves. Serve immediately.

Smoked Salmon Pump Bites

Submitted by Lindsay Podolak, TheNaughtyMommy.com. Looking for a fancy treat for your brunch table but have no time to cook? These little salmon bites look fancy but they are so easy to throw together.

INGREDIENTS | SERVES 8

8 gluten-free sandwich bread slices (or your favorite gluten-free cracker)

8 ounces chive and onion cream cheese

½ cup finely minced red onion

¼ cup capers

8 ounces smoked salmon

1. Preheat oven to 400°F.

2. Carefully remove the crusts from the bread slices and cut into 4 equal squares. Lay them on a baking sheet and toast in the oven for 5–7 minutes, until lightly browned. (If using crackers, there's no need to warm.)

3. When the bread slices are cool, spread each square with cream cheese, then top with minced onion and capers. Place smoked salmon pieces on top and serve.

Breadless Cheesy Garlic Bread

Submitted by Cindy Dudas from her blog, Whatever Works (http://whateverworks.typepad.com). Who needs the bread? Skip the middleman and put the cheese directly under the broiler to make these crispy treats. Enjoy them alone or alongside a plate of fried eggs and bacon.

INGREDIENTS | SERVES 2

½ cup shredded mozzarella cheese

⅛ teaspoon garlic powder

⅛ teaspoon dried oregano

⅛ cup grated Parmesan cheese

1. Spread the mozzarella into the bottom of a small ovenproof frying pan. Sprinkle the garlic powder and oregano evenly on top of the mozzarella cheese and top with the Parmesan.

2. Place the pan in the oven under the broiler until the cheese is bubby and lightly browned. Let it cool for 5 minutes and remove it on a single sheet. Cut into wedges with a pizza cutter and enjoy!

Chocolate Avocado Pudding

This recipe comes from Lesa, BearHavenMama.com. This pudding is delicious enough to serve as a dessert and nutritious enough to serve for breakfast.

INGREDIENTS | SERVES 2

2 ripe avocados

½ cup raw honey (or agave nectar)

½ cup cocoa powder

1 teaspoon pure vanilla extract

Mash the avocados in a bowl and then add to the blender. Blend until smooth. Add the rest of the ingredients and blend until smooth.

Breakfast Salad

Salad isn't just for lunch and dinner anymore. Try this mix of delicious ingredients in the morning for a boost in energy and nutrients.

INGREDIENTS | SERVES 2

3 cups baby spinach leaves

4 large eggs, hard-boiled, peeled, and quartered

2 slices bacon, cooked and chopped

½ cup cucumber, sliced

½ avocado, diced

½ apple, sliced

Juice of ½ lemon

Arrange the spinach leaves on a plate and top with the eggs and bacon. Add the cucumber, avocado, and apple slices to top of the salad. Drizzle with lemon juice. Serve immediately.

Antioxidant Fruit and Nut Salad

Fruit salad can be eaten any time of day, but is particularly good for breakfast. Berries are packed full of antioxidants and walnuts have one of the best omega profiles for nuts to reduce inflammation. This is a winning combination.

INGREDIENTS | SERVES 2

½ cup sliced strawberries

½ cup raspberries

½ cup blackberries

½ cup blueberries

½ cup dried mulberries

½ cup chopped walnuts

Combine all the ingredients in a bowl and enjoy.

Stuffed Tomatoes

This vegetarian brunch option is packed with flavor.

1. Preheat oven to 350°F.

2. Hollow out the tomatoes, reserving the tomato pulp. Place the tomatoes in a small baking dish.

3. Mix the tomato pulp with the mushrooms, garlic, sun-dried tomatoes, pepper, paprika, thyme, and basil.

4. Fill the tomatoes with the tomato pulp mixture and bake for 25 minutes.

CHAPTER 12

Slow Cooker Breakfast Favorites

Gluten-Free Breakfast Granola

Finding gluten-free granola can be a challenge in most grocery stores, but it's super easy to make your own in the slow cooker. Make sure to stir the ingredients about every 30 minutes to prevent uneven cooking or overbrowning.

INGREDIENTS | SERVES 10

2½ cups gluten-free old-fashioned rolled oats

¼ cup ground flaxseeds

½ cup unsweetened shredded coconut

½ cup pumpkin seeds

½ cup chopped walnuts

½ cup sliced almonds

1 cup dried cranberries

¾ packed cup light brown sugar

⅓ cup coconut oil

¼ cup honey

½ teaspoon salt

1 teaspoon ground cinnamon

Change It Up

Don't like pumpkin seeds, walnuts, or dried cranberries? Use the seeds, nuts, and dried fruit that you prefer in your own granola. Use raisins, sunflower seeds, cocoa nibs, dried cranberries, or even dried bananas. The different variations are endless. You can even add chocolate chips if you'd like, but only after the granola has been cooked and cooled!

1. Mix together all the ingredients and place in a greased 4-quart slow cooker.

2. Cover the slow cooker and vent with a wooden spoon handle or a chopstick. Cook on high for 4 hours, or on low for 8 hours, stirring every hour or so.

3. When the granola is toasty and done, pour it onto a cookie sheet that has been lined with parchment paper. Spread out the granola evenly over the entire sheet of parchment paper. Allow the granola to cool and dry for several hours.

4. Once cooled, break up the granola and place in an airtight container or a tightly sealed glass jar and store in the pantry for up to 1 month. For longer storage keep the granola in the freezer for up to 6 months.

Chunky Applesauce

Apples are so versatile in the slow cooker. Use whatever type of apples you prefer for this recipe. Serve as a side dish to pork, chicken, or beef or just as a snack paired with a handful of your favorite nuts or seeds.

INGREDIENTS | SERVES 6

3–5 pounds apples
2 tablespoons lemon juice

Need Some Sugar?

Apples are more or less sweet depending on their variety. If you'd like to sweeten your applesauce, start by adding ¼ cup of your favorite sweetener as soon as the apples have finished cooking: sugar, honey, agave nectar, concentrated fruit juice or apple cider, or even molasses will work.

1. Peel, core, and roughly dice the apples. You should have about 10 cups of uncooked, diced apples.

2. Place the apples and lemon juice in a greased 2.5-quart or 4-quart slow cooker. Cook on high for 4 hours or on low for 7–8 hours. The apples are done when they are easily mashed with a fork.

3. Mash the cooked apples in the slow cooker until they are a chunky consistency. Cool for 30 minutes and then refrigerate in an airtight container.

Ham and Cheese Omelet

Eggs are one of the most affordable proteins available and they are naturally gluten-free. If you make a large family-size omelet like this on Sunday evening, you'll have ready-made breakfasts for the rest of the week.

INGREDIENTS | SERVES 5

10 large eggs
½ teaspoon dry mustard
½ teaspoon salt
½ teaspoon paprika
½ teaspoon ground black pepper
½ teaspoon dill weed
1½ cups diced ham
1½ cups shredded Cheddar cheese
½ cup chopped green onions

1. Whisk the eggs in a large bowl. Add the mustard, salt, paprika, pepper, and dill weed. Stir in the diced ham.

2. Pour the egg mixture into a greased 2.5-quart slow cooker.

3. Sprinkle the cheese and green onions over the top of the egg mixture. Cover and cook on high for 1½–2 hours or on low for 2½–3 hours.

How to Store Fresh Green Onions

Green onions have small white bulbs and long green stalks. Both parts of the onion can be eaten. They are also referred to as spring onions and scallions. Either way, they will often go bad if left in the refrigerator. The best way to preserve them is to buy two or three bunches, slice them all up and place them in the freezer in a resealable plastic bag from which the air has been removed. They will stay fresh and can be used right from the freezer.

Blackberry French Toast Casserole

Store-bought gluten-free bread is too expensive to waste if it becomes stale. This recipe shows you how to make a frugal but delicious breakfast or dessert using leftover or stale gluten-free bread. Serve this indulgent treat with butter and maple syrup or dust with powdered sugar and top with softly whipped cream.

INGREDIENTS | SERVES 6

7 cups cubed gluten-free bread

1⅓ cups whole milk

5 large eggs, whisked

1 tablespoon vanilla extract

1 tablespoon maple syrup

½ teaspoon salt

2 tablespoons butter or coconut oil, melted

2 teaspoons ground cinnamon

3 tablespoons granulated sugar

1½ cups blackberries, fresh or frozen

1. In a large bowl, mix together the bread, milk, eggs, vanilla, maple syrup, and salt.

2. Pour the mixture into a greased 4-quart slow cooker.

3. Drizzle the melted butter or coconut oil over the casserole. Sprinkle the cinnamon and sugar evenly over the bread. Top with blackberries.

4. Cover the slow cooker and vent with a wooden spoon handle or chopstick. Cook on high for 2½–3 hours or on low for 5–6 hours.

5. Remove the lid and allow the liquid to evaporate the last 20 minutes of cooking. Serve warm.

Spanish Tortilla

Traditionally served as tapas or an appetizer in Spanish restaurants and bars, this version of the Spanish tortilla makes a healthy breakfast casserole. Conventionally it does not contain cheese, but feel free to sprinkle some on top in the last 30 minutes of cooking.

INGREDIENTS | SERVES 6

2 small yellow onions, finely diced

3 tablespoons olive oil

10 large eggs

1 teaspoon salt

1 teaspoon ground black pepper

3 large baking potatoes, peeled and thinly sliced

1. In a skillet over medium heat, slowly cook the onions in the olive oil until lightly brown and caramelized, about 5–6 minutes.

2. In a large bowl, whisk together the eggs, salt, and pepper.

3. Layer half of the potatoes and fried onions in a greased 4-quart slow cooker. Pour half the eggs over the layers. Repeat the layers, ending with the last of the whisked eggs.

4. Cover and cook on low for 6–7 hours or on high for 3½–4 hours.

Cheesy Grits Casserole

Cheesy grits is a favorite dish to bring to potlucks. This recipe combines eggs, bacon, and cheesy grits all in a single pot.

INGREDIENTS | SERVES 8

1½ cups Bob's Red Mill Gluten Free Corn Grits (also known as "polenta style;" not quick-cooking)

4¼ cups water

1 teaspoon salt

½ teaspoon ground black pepper

4 tablespoons butter, divided

6 large eggs

1 pound bacon, cooked and crumbled

1 cup shredded Cheddar cheese

1. Combine the grits, water, salt, pepper, and 2 tablespoons of butter in a greased 4-quart slow cooker.

2. Cover and cook on high for 3 hours or on low for 6 hours.

3. Thirty minutes before serving, whisk the eggs in a large bowl and cook them in a medium saucepan over medium heat in the remaining 2 tablespoons butter for 4–5 minutes or until cooked through. Fold the scrambled eggs into the cooked grits in the slow cooker. Add the crumbled bacon and cheese.

4. Cook on high for an additional 30 minutes to melt the cheese and heat the bacon through.

Crustless Quiche Lorraine

Ham is often already salty, so take that into consideration when deciding how much salt you add to the egg mixture. The gluten-free bread "crust" in this recipe is also optional; the quiche is just as delicious without it.

INGREDIENTS | SERVES 4

4 slices gluten-free bread, toasted
4 teaspoons butter, divided
2 cups grated Swiss cheese
½ pound cooked ham, cut into cubes
6 large eggs
1 tablespoon mayonnaise
½ teaspoon Dijon mustard
1 cup heavy cream
½ teaspoon salt
½ teaspoon freshly ground pepper
⅛ teaspoon cayenne pepper

1. Grease a 4-quart slow cooker with nonstick spray. If desired, remove the crusts from the gluten-free toast. Butter each slice with 1 teaspoon of butter, tear the toast into pieces, and arrange the toast pieces butter-side down in the slow cooker.

2. Spread half of the cheese over the toast pieces, and then spread the ham over the cheese, and top the ham layer with the remaining cheese.

3. In a bowl, beat the eggs with the mayonnaise, mustard, cream, salt, black pepper, and cayenne pepper. Pour the egg mixture into the slow cooker.

4. Cover and cook on high for 1½–2 hours or on low for 3–4 hours until the eggs are set.

Eggs Florentine

Freshly ground black pepper goes well in this dish. You can use up to 1 teaspoon in the recipe. If you prefer to go lighter on the seasoning to accommodate individual tastes, be sure to have a pepper grinder at the table for those who want to add more.

INGREDIENTS | SERVES 4

2 cups grated Cheddar cheese, divided

1 (10-ounce) package frozen spinach, thawed

1 (8-ounce) can sliced mushrooms, drained

1 small onion, peeled and diced

6 large eggs

1 cup heavy cream

½ teaspoon Italian seasoning

½ teaspoon garlic powder

½ teaspoon freshly ground black pepper

Make It Dairy-Free

To make egg casseroles dairy-free, replace the cream with full-fat coconut milk. For the Cheddar cheese, there are many dairy-free alternatives available now; one in particular, called Daiya, is sold in shreds and melts beautifully in dishes like this.

1. Grease a 4-quart slow cooker with butter. Spread 1 cup of the grated cheese over the bottom of the slow cooker.

2. Drain the spinach and squeeze out any excess moisture; add in a layer on top of the cheese. Next add the drained mushrooms in a layer and then top them with the onion.

3. In a small bowl, beat together the eggs, cream, Italian seasoning, garlic powder, and pepper. Pour over the layers in the slow cooker. Top with the remaining cup of cheese.

4. Cover and cook on high for 2 hours or until the eggs are set.

Breakfast Quinoa with Fruit

Any dried fruit can be used in this dish. Experiment with a few different kinds and see which you like best!

INGREDIENTS | SERVES 4

1 cup quinoa, rinsed and drained
2 cups water
½ cup dried mixed berries
1 pear, thinly sliced and peeled if desired
½ packed cup dark brown sugar
½ teaspoon ground ginger
¼ teaspoon ground cinnamon
⅛ teaspoon ground cloves
⅛ teaspoon ground nutmeg

Stir together all the ingredients in a 4-quart slow cooker. Cook for 2½ hours on high or about 4 hours on low, or until the quinoa has absorbed most of the liquid and is light and fluffy.

What Is Quinoa?

Pronounced "keen-wah," this crop is grown as a grain, although it's actually a seed. It's become very popular in recent years, being touted as a health food. The grain itself has been used for thousands of years in South America. It's a perfect addition to the gluten-free diet because of its high nutritional content. It is important to rinse and drain before cooking with quinoa to remove the saponin, a natural coating that can make it taste bitter or soapy.

Pumpkin Oatmeal

Pop this into your slow cooker before you go to bed and wake up in the morning to the delightful scent of pumpkin wafting through your house. This recipe is the perfect breakfast for a chilly autumn day.

INGREDIENTS | SERVES 6

1 cup gluten-free steel-cut oats (such as Bob's Red Mill)
2 cups whole milk
⅓ packed cup light brown sugar
½ cup butter, melted
1 teaspoon vanilla extract
2 teaspoons pumpkin pie spice

1. In a large bowl, mix together all the ingredients. Pour into a greased 4-quart slow cooker.

2. Cook on low for 8 hours. Serve warm with a sprinkle of cinnamon sugar on top.

Pull-Apart Cinnamon Raisin Biscuits

Whoever thought you could make gluten-free biscuits in the slow cooker? Well you can, and they turn out light and soft with a perfect crumb! To prevent the biscuits on the edge from browning too quickly, line the slow cooker with parchment paper.

INGREDIENTS | SERVES 9

1 cup brown rice flour

1 cup arrowroot starch

1 tablespoon baking powder

1 teaspoon xanthan gum

½ teaspoon salt

⅓ cup granulated sugar

½ teaspoon ground cinnamon

⅓ cup gluten-free vegetable shortening such as Crisco

2 large eggs

¾ cup whole milk

½ cup raisins

Quick Vanilla Glaze

Impress your family by making a quick powdered sugar glaze for these lightly sweetened biscuits/buns. Mix together 1 cup of powdered sugar with 1½ table-spoons of water or milk and ½ teaspoon of vanilla extract. Drizzle artistically over warm buns and serve immediately.

1. In a large bowl, whisk together the brown rice flour, arrowroot starch, baking powder, xanthan gum, salt, sugar, and cinnamon.

2. Cut in the vegetable shortening using a fork and knife until it resembles small peas within the flour mixture.

3. In a small bowl, whisk together the eggs and milk. Pour into the flour mixture and mix with a fork to combine until the dough is like a very thick, sticky cake batter. Fold in the raisins.

4. Grease a 4-quart slow cooker and/or line with parchment paper.

5. Drop biscuit dough in balls about the size of a golf ball into the bottom of the slow cooker. The biscuits will touch each other and may fit quite snugly.

6. Cover the slow cooker and vent the lid with the handle of a wooden spoon or a chopstick. Cook the biscuits on high for about 2–2½ hours or on low for about 4–4½ hours. Biscuits around the edge of the slow cooker will be more brown than those in the center. The biscuits should have doubled in size during cooking. The biscuits are done when a toothpick inserted in the center of the middle biscuit comes out clean.

7. Turn the slow cooker off and remove the insert to a heat-safe surface such as the stovetop or on top of potholders. Allow the biscuits to cool for several minutes before removing from the slow cooker insert. They will "pull-apart" individually.

Pear Clafoutis

Clafoutis is a soft, pancake-like breakfast with fruit. If you choose to use a larger slow cooker than the specified 2.5-quart, you will need to reduce the cooking time. When the sides are golden brown and a toothpick stuck in the middle comes out clean, the clafoutis is done.

INGREDIENTS | SERVES 4

2 pears, stem and seeds removed, cut into chunks, and peeled if preferred

½ cup brown rice flour

½ cup arrowroot starch

2 teaspoons baking powder

½ teaspoon xanthan gum

¼ teaspoon salt

⅓ cup granulated sugar

1 teaspoon ground cinnamon

2 tablespoons butter, melted

2 large eggs

¾ cup whole milk

1 tablespoon vanilla extract

1. Place the pears in a greased 2.5-quart slow cooker.

2. In a large bowl, whisk together the brown rice flour, arrowroot starch, baking powder, xanthan gum, salt, sugar, and cinnamon.

3. Make a well in the center of the dry ingredients and add the butter, eggs, milk, and vanilla. Stir to combine the wet and dry ingredients.

4. Pour the batter over the pears. Cover the slow cooker and vent the lid with a chopstick or the handle of a wooden spoon.

5. Cook on high for 2½–3 hours or on low for 5–6 hours. Serve warm or cold drizzled with maple syrup.

Gluten-Free Baking Shortcut

Don't want to mix up all these ingredients? You can replace the brown rice flour, arrowroot starch, baking powder, and xanthan gum with 1 cup of Bob's Red Mill Gluten Free Pancake Mix or your favorite gluten-free pancake mix.

Millet Porridge with Apples and Pecans

Millet, like quinoa, is a small seed cereal crop that is perfect for the gluten-free diet. It's very easy to digest and makes a healthy hot breakfast.

INGREDIENTS | SERVES 4

4 cups whole milk

1 cup dried millet

1 apple, diced (and peeled if preferred)

2 teaspoons ground cinnamon

½ cup honey

½ cup chopped pecans

¼ teaspoon salt

1. Grease a 2.5-quart slow cooker with butter.

2. Add all the ingredients to the slow cooker and stir to mix.

3. Cook on high for 2½–3 hours or on low for 5–6 hours, until all the liquid has been absorbed into the millet. Try not to overcook, as it can become mushy.

A Note on Millet

Millet is particularly high in magnesium, which is a common deficiency in many with celiac disease. It also seems to help lower triglycerides and C-reactive protein (an inflammatory marker important in assessing cardiovascular risk).

Cheesy Hash Brown Casserole

This is a perfect slow cooker recipe that is easy to put together the night before. Place it in the refrigerator and it can be slow cooked for a little over 2 hours on high in the morning.

INGREDIENTS | SERVES 4

26 ounces shredded hash browns, squeezed dry of all water

2 large eggs

2 cups shredded Cheddar cheese, divided

1 cup mayonnaise

¼ cup chopped yellow onion

½ cup melted butter, divided

1½ cups crushed gluten-free Rice Chex Cereal

1. Grease a 2.5- or 4-quart slow cooker.

2. In a large bowl, mix together the drained hash browns, eggs, 1½ cups cheese, mayonnaise, onion, and ¼ cup melted butter. Pour into the slow cooker.

3. In small bowl, stir together the Rice Chex, the remaining melted butter, and the remaining cheese. Spread the topping evenly over the hash browns. Cover the slow cooker and vent the lid with a chopstick or the handle of a wooden spoon.

4. Cook on high for 2½ hours or on low for 4 hours, until the casserole is cooked through and firm and the cheese has melted on the top.

"Baked" Apples

Serve these lightly spiced apples as a simple dessert or a breakfast treat.

INGREDIENTS | SERVES 6

6 baking apples, peeled, and thickly sliced

½ cup water

1 cinnamon stick

1" knob peeled fresh ginger

1 vanilla bean

Baking with Apples

When baking, choose apples with firm flesh such as Granny Smith, Jonathan, McIntosh, Cortland, Pink Lady, Pippin, or Winesap. They will be able to hold up to long cooking times without turning to mush. Leaving the skin on adds fiber.

1. Place the apples in a single layer in the bottom of a 4- or 6-quart slow cooker. Add the water, cinnamon stick, ginger, and vanilla bean. Cook on low for 6–8 hours or until the apples are tender and easily pierced with a fork.

2. Use a slotted spoon to remove the apples from the slow cooker. Discard the cinnamon stick, ginger, vanilla bean, and water. Serve hot.

Peachy Cinnamon Bread Pudding

Peaches, sugar, cinnamon, and gluten-free toast come together to make a delicious morning breakfast casserole.

INGREDIENTS | SERVES 4

4 cups gluten-free bread cubes, toasted

1 cup granulated sugar

½ teaspoon ground cinnamon

4 large eggs, beaten

1½ cups whole milk

1 tablespoon vanilla extract

1½ cups peeled and sliced fresh peaches

⅓ cup butter, melted

2 tablespoons granulated sugar mixed with 1 teaspoon cinnamon

1. In a large bowl, mix together the bread cubes, sugar, cinnamon, eggs, milk, and vanilla. Fold in the peaches.

2. Pour the mixture into a greased 4-quart slow cooker. Drizzle the butter over the casserole. Sprinkle the cinnamon and sugar over the butter.

3. Cook on high for 3–4 hours or on low for 6–8 hours, until the eggs are set.

Breakfast Risotto

Serve this as you would cooked oatmeal: topped with additional brown sugar, raisins or other dried fruit, and milk.

INGREDIENTS | SERVES 6

¼ cup butter, melted

1½ cups Arborio rice

3 small apples, peeled, cored, and sliced

1½ teaspoons ground cinnamon

⅛ teaspoon freshly ground nutmeg

⅛ teaspoon ground cloves

⅛ teaspoon salt

⅓ packed cup light brown sugar

1 cup apple juice

3 cups whole milk

Arborio Rice

Arborio rice is a short-grain rice used in risotto because it has a creamy texture when cooked. Other varieties used in risotto are vialone nano and carnaroli rice.

1. Add the butter and rice to a greased 4-quart slow cooker; stir to coat the rice in the butter.

2. Add the remaining ingredients and stir to combine. Cover and cook on low for 6–7 hours or on high for 2–3 hours, until the rice is cooked through and firm but not mushy.

Apple and Pear Spread

Make the most of in-season apples and pears in this easy alternative to apple or pear butter.

INGREDIENTS | YIELDS 1 QUART

4 Winesap apples, cored, sliced, and peeled

4 Bartlett pears, cored, sliced, and peeled

1 cup water or pear cider

¼ packed cup light brown sugar

¼ cup granulated sugar

¼ teaspoon ground ginger

¼ teaspoon ground cinnamon

¼ teaspoon ground nutmeg

¼ teaspoon ground allspice

1. Mix together all the ingredients in a 4-quart slow cooker. Cook on low for 10–12 hours.

2. Uncover and cook on low for an additional 1–2 hours or until thick and most of the liquid has evaporated.

3. Allow to cool completely, then pour into the food processor and purée. Pour into clean glass jars. Refrigerate up to 6 weeks.

Do-It-Yourself Brown Sugar

Brown sugar is simply white sugar that has been mixed with molasses. Make brown sugar by combining 1 cup granulated sugar with ¼ cup molasses. Store in an airtight container.

Chorizo and Potato Casserole

If you don't have Mexican chorizo sausage available in your local grocery store, use mild breakfast sausage instead.

INGREDIENTS | SERVES 6

⅓ cup olive oil

1 small yellow onion, diced

3 medium Yukon gold potatoes, peeled and cut into ½" cubes

8 ounces Mexican chorizo sausage, removed from casing

8 large eggs

¼ teaspoon salt

¼ teaspoon ground black pepper

1. In a heavy skillet, heat the olive oil on medium until sizzling. Add the onion and cook for 3–5 minutes, until soft.

2. Add the potatoes and cook for another 5–8 minutes, until the potatoes are fork tender. Using a large slotted spoon, transfer the potato mixture to a bowl and set aside.

3. In the same skillet, brown the chorizo over medium heat until cooked through, about 5–7 minutes.

4. Grease a 4-quart slow cooker. Layer the potato mixture with the cooked chorizo in the slow cooker.

5. In a large bowl, mix together the eggs, salt, and pepper. Evenly pour over the layered ingredients.

6. Cook on high for 3–4 hours or on low for 6–8 hours, until the eggs are set. If necessary, add salt and pepper to taste when serving.

Coconut Milk Yogurt

If you're intolerant to dairy proteins like casein or dairy sugar (lactose), this coconut milk yogurt is a perfect alternative that you can make right in your slow cooker! Serve the yogurt plain or with any flavor jam or fresh fruit.

INGREDIENTS | SERVES 8

6 cups full-fat coconut milk

6 capsules of allergen-free probiotics or yogurt starter

3 tablespoons plain gelatin

½ cup granulated sugar, optional

½ cup blackberry jam, optional

Using Probiotics to Make Yogurt

You will need to purchase a yogurt starter or probiotics that contain "live active cultures" to create this yogurt. Alternately, if you have a grocery store nearby that sells yogurt made from coconut milk, you can simply purchase a small container of plain coconut milk yogurt and use that as your starter instead of using probiotic capsules.

1. Pour the coconut milk into a 4-quart slow cooker. Turn the slow cooker on low and cook for 3 hours.

2. Turn the slow cooker off and let it sit for 3 hours. (Cooking the mixture first will help to kill off any bad bacteria that may be in the coconut milk.) Once the coconut milk has cooled, after 3 hours, remove 1 cup of the warm coconut milk and mix it in a glass bowl with the contents of the probiotics capsules and the gelatin.

3. Return the probiotic/coconut milk mixture to the slow cooker. Whisk thoroughly to distribute the probiotics and gelatin throughout the mixture. Place the lid back on the slow cooker.

4. Leave the slow cooker turned off, but wrap the slow cooker in several layers of bath towels to give the probiotics a warm environment to grow. Leave the towel-wrapped slow cooker alone for 8–10 hours.

5. After 8 hours, stir in the sugar if desired and place the covered slow cooker insert into the refrigerator. Allow the yogurt to chill for 6–8 hours. This will allow the gelatin to thicken the yogurt so it has the proper texture. Serve cold topped with blackberry jam, if desired.

Buttermilk Drop Biscuits

Buttermilk adds a tangy flavor to these fluffy gluten-free biscuits.

INGREDIENTS | YIELDS 10–12

2 cups brown rice flour

¼ cup sorghum flour

½ cup arrowroot starch

¼ cup potato starch or cornstarch

2 tablespoons granulated sugar

4 teaspoons baking powder

1 teaspoon salt

1 teaspoon baking soda

1 teaspoon xanthan gum

½ cup chilled butter

1¼ cups buttermilk

1 large egg

Dairy-Free "Buttermilk"

For a dairy-free buttermilk alternative, mix 2 tablespoons of lemon juice or apple cider vinegar with 1¼ cups almond milk or coconut milk.

1. In a large bowl, mix together all the dry ingredients. Cut the butter into the dry ingredients with two knives or with a pastry cutter until it resembles small peas throughout the dry ingredients.

2. In a smaller bowl, whisk together the buttermilk and egg. Pour the buttermilk mixture into the dry ingredients and mix with a fork. The dough will be slightly stiff when thoroughly mixed.

3. Line a 6-quart slow cooker with parchment paper and spray it with nonstick cooking spray.

4. Using an ice-cream scoop, scoop out 10–12 drop biscuits and place them on the parchment paper on the bottom of the slow cooker.

5. Cover and vent the lid of the slow cooker with a chopstick or the end of a wooden spoon. Cook on high for 2–2½ hours, until the biscuits have risen by about half and are cooked through.

Baked Stuffed Apples

Serve these baked apples with coffee cake for breakfast.

INGREDIENTS | SERVES 4

4 large tart baking apples

½ packed cup light brown sugar

4 teaspoons grated orange zest

1 teaspoon ground cinnamon

¼ cup golden seedless raisins, divided

4 teaspoons frozen orange juice concentrate, divided

4 teaspoons butter, divided

½ cup apple cider or juice

1. Wash the apples and remove the cores and the stems, but don't peel them.

2. Add the brown sugar, orange zest, and cinnamon to a small bowl; stir to mix.

3. Fill each apple with 1 tablespoon raisins, 1 teaspoon orange juice concentrate, and 1 generous tablespoon of the brown sugar mixture. Top the filling in each apple with 1 teaspoon butter.

4. Pour the cider or juice into the slow cooker. Carefully place the apples upright in the slow cooker. Cover and cook on low for 5 hours or until the apples are cooked through and tender.

5. Use tongs and a spatula to remove the apples to dessert plates. Serve warm.

Sausage and Egg Breakfast Casserole

Start this heating in the slow cooker before you go to bed and wake up in the morning to a nice, warm breakfast casserole! It's perfect for those busy mornings before school.

INGREDIENTS | SERVES 6

8 large eggs, gently beaten

1 large Idaho potato, shredded

1 pound pork sausage, crumbled

1 small yellow onion, diced

½ green bell pepper, diced

1 garlic clove, minced

2 teaspoons dried basil

½ teaspoon salt

¼ teaspoon ground black pepper

1. Grease a 4- or 6-quart slow cooker with butter.

2. In a large bowl, mix together all the ingredients thoroughly. Add to the slow cooker and cook on low for 8 hours. Serve warm.

Breakfast Burrito Filling

Wrap cooked ingredients in egg whites (pan-fried and formed to a size similar to a tortilla), and serve with your favorite breakfast burrito toppings.

INGREDIENTS | SERVES 4

1¼ pounds lean boneless pork, cubed

12 ounces diced tomatoes with green chilies

1 small onion, diced

1 jalapeño, diced

½ teaspoon ground chipotle

¼ teaspoon cayenne pepper

¼ teaspoon ground jalapeño

2 cloves garlic, minced

Place all the ingredients into a 2-quart slow cooker. Stir. Cook on low for 8 hours. Stir before serving.

"Hard-Boiled" Eggs

This old-fashioned, hard-boiled breakfast "staple" has never been so simply prepared.

INGREDIENTS | SERVES 12

12 large eggs

1. Place the eggs in a 6-quart slow cooker. Cook on high for 2 hours.

2. Gently remove the eggs and place in a bowl of ice water (this loosens the shell for peeling). Peel and enjoy!

Slow-Cooked Scrambler

Preparing a warm and hearty scrambled egg dish is a breeze in the slow cooker. A delicious start to the day.

INGREDIENTS | SERVES 2

1 tablespoon canola oil

6 large eggs

6 tablespoons coconut milk

¼ teaspoon ground black pepper

Seasonings of choice, to taste (try dill, parsley, and scallions or your favorite herb combination)

1 cup chopped vegetables of choice (e.g., mushrooms, onions, peppers)

1 teaspoon minced garlic

1 teaspoon dry mustard

1. Heat the oil in a 4-quart slow cooker on low. Grease the sides of the slow cooker with additional oil, as needed.

2. In a medium bowl, whisk together the eggs, coconut milk, pepper, and seasonings.

3. Add the vegetables, garlic, and mustard and mix.

4. Transfer the egg mixture to the slow cooker, cover, and cook on low for 1 hour.

5. Stir the eggs with a fork to help break them up to cook evenly. Cook the scrambled eggs, covered, for 1 more hour. Stir the eggs again with a fork.

Cinnamon Stewed Plums

Serve as a breakfast fruit or as a dessert with a whipped topping.

INGREDIENTS | SERVES 4

½ cup honey

1 cup water

⅛ teaspoon salt

1 tablespoon fresh lemon juice

1 cinnamon stick

1 pound fresh, ripe plums (about 8 small or 6 medium), pitted

Combine all the ingredients in a 2- to 4-quart slow cooker and cook on low for about 6 hours, until the plums are tender. Serve warm, chilled, or at room temperature.

Ground Chicken and Carrot Quiche

This high-protein recipe can be served for breakfast, lunch, or dinner.

INGREDIENTS | SERVES 2

6 large eggs

½ pound ground chicken, browned

1 cup shredded carrots

½ cup beef broth

¼ cup chopped fresh parsley

½ teaspoon ground coriander

1. Grease the bottom and sides of a 2- to 4-quart slow cooker with coconut oil.

2. In a medium bowl beat the eggs well with a wire whisk. Add all the remaining ingredients and stir.

3. Add the egg mixture to the slow cooker, cover, and cook on low for 1 hour.

4. Stir the eggs with a fork to help break them up for even cooking. Cover, and cook on low for 1 more hour. Fluff with a fork and serve warm.

Southwestern Breakfast Bake

Perfect for brunch or a late breakfast for a special occasion with family or friends, as this dish takes a minimum of 4 hours to cook.

INGREDIENTS | SERVES 8

8 large eggs

1 (7-ounce) can diced green chilies, drained

2 cups coconut milk

1 cup sliced button mushrooms

1 red bell pepper, seeded and diced

1 small yellow onion, diced

1 cup diced tomatoes

¾ teaspoon lemon juice

½ teaspoon ground black pepper

2 (10-ounce) packages frozen spinach, thawed, undrained

1. Combine all the ingredients except the spinach in a bowl and whisk together.

2. Layer ⅓ of the spinach (about 3 ounces) in the bottom of 4-quart slow cooker. Pour ½ of the egg mixture on top of the spinach. Put another layer of spinach (about 3 ounces) on top of the egg mixture and top with the remaining egg mixture. Top with the remaining spinach.

3. Cover and cook on low for 6–7 hours or on high for 4–5 hours.

4. Uncover a few minutes before serving and cook on high to allow the finished product to dry out.

Paleo-Approved Zucchini Nut Bread

Top this sweet bread with some apple butter, peach marmalade, or other fruit spread.

INGREDIENTS | SERVES 8

3 large eggs, beaten

½ cup sunflower oil

½ cup unsweetened applesauce

1 teaspoon orange extract

¼ cup honey

2 teaspoons baking soda

1 teaspoon baking powder

1 teaspoon ground cinnamon

1 cup hazelnuts, ground to the consistency of coarse meal

1 cup pecans, ground to the consistency of coarse meal

1 cup almond powder

1 cup chopped walnut pieces

¾ pound zucchini, grated

1. Preheat a round 5-quart slow cooker with the lid on at high for 15 minutes.

2. Blend the egg, sunflower oil, applesauce, orange extract, honey, baking soda, baking powder, and cinnamon in a large bowl. Stir in the nuts and zucchini.

3. Spray the bottom and lower sides of the preheated slow cooker with the cooking spray.

4. Pour the batter evenly into the slow cooker. Cover and bake for 45–60 minutes, or until the bread pulls away from the sides of the slow cooker and the tip of a knife inserted into the center, held for 5 seconds, comes out clean.

Rubble Porridge

This Stone Age–inspired hot cereal is loaded with fiber, vitamin E, and omega-3 fatty acids.

INGREDIENTS | SERVES 6

½ cup raisins and cranberries
¼ cup slivered almonds
¼ cup raw pumpkin seeds
¼ cup raw sunflower seeds
¼ cup unsweetened coconut
⅛ cup honey
2 tablespoons coconut butter, melted

1. Place all the dry ingredients in a 4-quart slow cooker, drizzle with the honey and butter, and toss well.

2. Cover, vent the lid with a chopstick, and cook on high for 2½–3½ hours, stirring periodically to prevent burning.

3. Cool the porridge on parchment paper. Enjoy with almond or coconut milk.

CHAPTER 13

Smoothies

Apple, Pear, and Banana Green Smoothie

Don't even bother peeling and coring the apples and pears. Just throw everything in the blender!

INGREDIENTS | SERVES 2

1 ripe pear, quartered

1 medium-size sweet apple (such as Gala or Fuji), quartered

2 frozen bananas

1 cup mixed fresh greens (such as collards greens, kale, or spinach)

2 cups water

1–2 cups ice cubes

Combine all the ingredients in a blender and blend until smooth. Serve immediately.

Keep Frozen Bananas Handy

Peel browning bananas and place them in resealable plastic bags in the freezer. Then you'll have frozen bananas anytime you need them!

Chocolate–Peanut Butter Smoothie

This smoothie is so delicious you won't even believe it's healthy!

INGREDIENTS | SERVES 2

2 tablespoons unsweetened cocoa powder

2 tablespoons natural creamy peanut butter

½ frozen banana

½ cup almond milk (or milk of your choice)

½ cup low-fat plain Greek yogurt

½ teaspoon vanilla extract

4–5 ice cubes

Combine all the ingredients in a blender and blend until thick and creamy. Serve immediately.

Peach Smoothie

This refreshing smoothie is a decadent summertime treat. Peach skins are optional. If you have a heavy-duty blender, they will blend right in and give you the benefit of extra fiber. If your blender can't handle the skins, either peel and discard, or strain the smoothie before serving.

INGREDIENTS | SERVES 2

2 peaches, sliced (peelings are optional)

1 frozen banana, cut into chunks

1 peeled orange

½ packed cup baby spinach leaves (optional, but adds a nutritional punch)

1 cup whole milk or coconut milk

1 tablespoon honey

Combine all the ingredients in a blender and blend until smooth. Serve immediately.

Cranberry Orange Smoothie

Submitted by Alexandra Maul, MadetoGlow.com. This smoothie is the perfect combination of tart and sweet. It's also incredibly good for you—full of vitamin C, fiber, and an awesome array of phytonutrients.

INGREDIENTS | SERVES 1

½ cup fresh cranberries

1 large frozen banana

1 large orange, peeled

½ cup unsweetened coconut milk from a carton, not a can (canned is thicker)

5 ice cubes

Add all the ingredients to blender and process until smooth and creamy. If it is too tart for your taste, feel free to add 1 teaspoon of honey or maple syrup.

Banana Chocolate Smoothie

This smoothie can be adapted to suit your taste. Feel free to leave out the egg yolk if you're not comfortable with raw eggs. The coconut oil is optional as well; it's included more for the nutritional value than added flavor.

INGREDIENTS | SERVES 2

1 cup vanilla yogurt

2 egg yolks (optional)

1 cup whole milk

1 large frozen banana, cut into chunks

2 tablespoons unrefined coconut oil (optional)

2 heaping tablespoons cocoa powder

1 cup ice cubes

Combine all the ingredients in a blender and process until smooth. Serve immediately.

Creamy Tropical Smoothie

Submitted by Jessica Cohen, EatSleepBe.com, this smoothie brings the taste of the tropics right into your kitchen any time of year.

INGREDIENTS | SERVES 2

¾ cup coconut milk

1 frozen ripe banana, sliced

⅓ avocado

5 cubes frozen mango

5 cubes frozen papaya

2 teaspoons pure vanilla extract

Combine all the ingredients in a blender and process until smooth. Serve immediately.

Berry Agave Smoothie

Submitted by Jeremy Dabel of WholesomeDinnerTonight.blogspot.com. This smoothie is dairy-free, gluten-free, and packed with protein and fiber.

INGREDIENTS | SERVES 2

1½ cups frozen berry mix (blackberries, blueberries, raspberries)

1½ cups frozen strawberries

⅓ cup frozen mango chunks

2 tablespoons agave nectar or honey

2 tablespoons organic hemp protein powder (optional)

3 cups cold water

Combine all the ingredients in a blender and process until smooth. Serve immediately.

Gingerbread Spice Smoothie

This warming, spicy smoothie evokes the flavors and aroma of the holiday season while packing a hefty present of nutrition! Submitted by Dr. Jennifer L. Weinberg, MD, MPH, MBE, JenniferWeinbergMD.com.

INGREDIENTS | SERVES 1

1 cup baby spinach

1 cup whole milk or coconut milk

1 teaspoon pure vanilla extract

½ teaspoon ground cinnamon

¼ teaspoon ground nutmeg

½ teaspoon ground ginger

¼ teaspoon ground cardamom

1 tablespoon maple syrup

Place all the ingredients in a blender and process until creamy and smooth.

Triple Berry Smoothie

Submitted by Michelle Mayk.

INGREDIENTS | SERVES 2

1 cup frozen mixed berries

1 frozen ripe banana

8 ounces vanilla or strawberry yogurt

½ cup orange juice

½ cup vanilla ice cream

Place all the ingredients in a blender and process until creamy and smooth. Add honey for added sweetness if desired.

Fresh Fig Smoothie

Submitted by Alexandra Maul, MadetoGlow.com. The green figs add a lovely hint of sweetness and combine very well with the banana. The ginger is good for gastrointestinal support, but if you're not a fan of ginger, feel free to leave it out.

INGREDIENTS | SERVES 2

2 cups mixed fresh greens (such as baby spinach, chard, and kale)

½ cup coconut milk from a carton, not a can (canned is thicker), or your favorite milk product

5 large green figs

½ cucumber, sliced into large chunks

½" piece peeled ginger (optional)

1 large frozen banana, chopped into large chunks

Add all the ingredients to a blender and process until smooth.

Vegan Blackberry Coconut Smoothie

Submitted by Jessie Weaver, VanderbiltWife.com. This vegan smoothie is packed with healthy antioxidants.

INGREDIENTS | SERVES 2

1 (13.5-ounce) can coconut milk

1 pint blackberries

3 cups ice cubes

Juice and zest of 1 lime

Add all the ingredients to a blender and process until smooth.

Pumpkin Spice Green Smoothie

Submitted by Alexandra Maul, MadetoGlow.com. The frozen banana lends a wonderful creaminess and the frozen mango gives it a hint of sweetness without any added sugar.

INGREDIENTS | SERVES 1

1¼ cups unsweetened coconut milk from a carton, not a can (canned is thicker), or your favorite milk product

2 cups fresh spinach

¼ cup pumpkin purée

¼ cup frozen mango chunks

1 frozen banana, sliced

½ teaspoon vanilla extract

¼ teaspoon pumpkin pie spice

1 tablespoon pumpkin seeds or walnuts for garnish, optional

Add all the ingredients except the garnish to a blender and process until smooth. If you like it sweeter, add 1–2 teaspoons of honey or agave. Garnish with pumpkin seeds or walnuts, if desired.

Strawberry Smoothie

Submitted by Michelle Mayk. This refreshing smoothie tastes like summer, but you can enjoy it all year round by using frozen strawberries. In fact, it is better with frozen strawberries, as they give the smoothie that ideal thick, chilled consistency without watering it down with ice.

INGREDIENTS | SERVES 3

1 frozen banana, sliced

1½ cups frozen strawberries

½ cup milk

½ cup plain yogurt

¾ cup orange juice, freshly squeezed if possible

3 tablespoons honey (optional)

Add all the ingredients to a blender and process until smooth. Add honey for additional sweetness if desired.

Green Honey Banana Smoothie

Submitted by Jessica Cohen, EatSleepBe.com. The avocados in this smoothie are a great source of healthy fats, and they add a creamy texture without any dairy.

INGREDIENTS | SERVES 3

2 cups coconut milk, from the carton

2 frozen bananas, sliced

1 avocado, peeled and pitted

2 teaspoons frozen spinach

2 tablespoons honey

2 teaspoons pure vanilla extract

½ cup ice

Add all the ingredients to a blender and process until smooth.

Carrot Top o' the Morning to You

Rich in beta-carotene, this smoothie blends romaine lettuce with tasty carrots and apples to give you a sweet start that can help you stay focused, provide lasting energy, and maintain healthy eyes and metabolism.

INGREDIENTS | YIELDS 1 QUART

2 cups romaine lettuce

3 carrots, peeled and cut into sticks small enough for the blender

1 apple, peeled and cored

1 cup water

1. Add the first 3 ingredients in the order listed to a blender.

2. Add the water slowly while blending until desired texture is achieved.

Orange You Glad You Got Up for This?

Packed with brain-stimulating and immunity-protecting vitamin C, this smoothie is a great option when everyone around you seems to be sick. Its power is intensified with the antioxidant-rich coconut milk.

INGREDIENTS | YIELDS 1 QUART

1 cup iceberg lettuce

3 oranges, peeled

½ cup coconut milk out of the carton

1. Blend the lettuce and oranges until just combined.

2. Add the coconut milk slowly while blending until the desired consistency is reached.

Vitamin C

Oranges are known for their immunity-building power, and rightfully so! By consuming oranges every day, the human body can fight off illnesses from the common cold to serious cancers and heart disease. You can thank the rich beta-carotenes and the vitamin C. An orange is a definite boost for health and longevity.

Great Grapefruit

The grapefruit and cucumber combine in this smoothie to offer a refreshing zing to your morning with vitamins and nutrients that will wake you up and keep you feeling fresh throughout the day!

INGREDIENTS | YIELDS 1 QUART

1 cup baby greens

2 grapefruits, peeled

1 cucumber, peeled and sliced

¼ cup water

1. Combine the greens, grapefruit, and cucumber with half of the water and blend.

2. Add the remaining water slowly while blending until desired consistency is reached.

Splendid Citrus

Booming with the strong flavors of pineapple, orange, grapefruit, lemon, and lime, this sweet and tart smoothie will liven up your senses while providing you with a boost in physical and mental health.

INGREDIENTS | YIELDS 1 QUART

2 large kale leaves

1 cup cubed pineapple

1 large orange or 2 small oranges, peeled

1 grapefruit, peeled

½ lemon, peeled

½ lime, peeled

1. Combine the kale and all the fruits in a blender in the order listed.

2. Blend until desired consistency is reached.

Raspberry Tart Morning Start

Raspberries and lime join to make a sweet and tart smoothie that will open your sinuses and sweeten your morning. This blend will please all of your taste buds!

INGREDIENTS | YIELDS 3 CUPS

1 cup plain Greek yogurt, divided
1 cup romaine lettuce
2 pints raspberries
½ lime, peeled

1. Pour ½ cup yogurt in a blender, followed by the romaine, raspberries, and lime. Blend.

2. Add the remaining yogurt while blending until desired texture is achieved.

Fight Cancer with Sweetness

With each providing a sweet and tart flavor, limes and raspberries are extremely powerful additions to any day. Rich in antioxidants and packing powerful anticancer properties, these two fruits pair up to keep your immune system running at its best.

Coconut Craziness

Adding the flesh of the coconut and the coconut milk to this smoothie results in a sweet flavor that complements the iceberg nicely. This smoothie will make you crave coconuts like crazy!

INGREDIENTS | YIELDS 3–4 CUPS

1 cup iceberg lettuce
Flesh of 2 coconuts (about 3–4 cups)
1 cup coconut milk, divided, out of the carton

1. Combine the lettuce, coconut flesh, and ½ cup coconut milk in a blender and blend.

2. Add the remaining coconut milk while blending until desired texture is achieved.

Coconut Power

In addition to being a staple in the diets of many countries, the coconut is held in high regard by many cultures for its medicinal abilities. Thought to cure and relieve the symptoms associated with many illnesses, the coconut, its flesh, its milk, and the oil that it can produce are packed with antioxidants and important vitamins and minerals.

Go Nutty!

Protein, protein, protein! In addition to the vitamins, minerals, and nutrients from the iceberg and banana, the protein from the almond milk and Greek yogurt make this smoothie a powerful start to any day.

INGREDIENTS | YIELDS 1 QUART

½ cup plain Greek yogurt

1 cup iceberg lettuce

1 frozen banana

1 cup vanilla-flavored almond milk, divided

1. Combine the yogurt, iceberg, and banana in a blender with ½ cup of almond milk and blend thoroughly.

2. Add the remaining almond milk while blending until desired consistency is reached.

Make Your Own Almond Milk

If you'd like to create your own almond milk, combine ½ cup water and 1 cup almonds and blend thoroughly. Strain before using. For vanilla almond milk, add a teaspoon of vanilla extract (or to taste).

Delicious Dandelion

A little-known green, the dandelion has been written off as a nuisance or weed. Although they can be quite bitter, the sweetness from the grapes, apple, and vanilla soy milk give this smoothie a very different taste that you're sure to enjoy!

INGREDIENTS | YIELDS 3 CUPS

1 cup dandelion greens

1 cup purple seedless grapes

1 sweet apple

1 cup vanilla soymilk

1. Place the dandelion greens, grapes, apple, and ½ cup soymilk in a blender and blend until thoroughly combined.

2. Add the remaining soymilk while blending until desired texture is achieved.

Benefits of Grapes

Although many people choose grapes as a snack because they're a low-calorie and sweet treat, the health benefits of grapes are a great reason to include them in your daily diet. Grapes contain powerful polyphenols that can help reduce the risk of heart disease and fight multiple types of cancer.

Pear Splendor

Pears give this smoothie its unique sweetness and taste while the banana adds a sweet, smooth texture. Packed with vitamins and nutrients, this smoothie is a sweet and tasty fiber-filled delight!

INGREDIENTS | YIELDS 3 CUPS

1 cup spinach
2 pears, cored and peeled
1 frozen banana
1 cup almond milk, divided

1. Combine the spinach, pears, banana, and ½ cup almond milk in a blender and blend until smooth.

2. While blending, add the remaining almond milk until desired texture is achieved.

A Sweet Beet to Step To

This deep-purple treat gets its color from the vibrant beets and deep-colored radicchio. Packed with vitamins A, B, C, E, and K, this already nutritious blend packs a protein punch as well with the creamy Greek yogurt.

INGREDIENTS | SERVES 1

1 cup radicchio
3 cups sliced beets
1 cup plain Greek yogurt, divided

1. Place the radicchio, beets, and ½ cup yogurt in a blender and blend to combine thoroughly.

2. While blending, add the remaining yogurt until desired texture is achieved.

Beets' Reddening Effects

If you are new to consuming beets, you should know that you will see some reddening in the smoothie, and more than you would expect. Although not a cause for concern, following beet consumption, urine may turn a slightly reddish or light purple color, most often found in people with deficient or excess amounts of iron.

Crazy Carrot

*Some may not believe a green vegetable smoothie could be sweet and delicious—
this smoothie is one for those nonbelievers. Crisp romaine, sweet carrots, and
smooth banana meet in this smoothie to provide a treat for your senses!*

INGREDIENTS | SERVES 2

1 cup romaine lettuce

3 carrots, peeled and cut into pieces
small enough to blend

1 frozen banana

½ cup vanilla or plain almond
milk, divided

1. Place the romaine, carrots, banana, and half of the almond milk in a blender and blend until thoroughly combined.

2. If needed, add the remaining almond milk while blending until desired consistency is reached.

Carrots, Bananas, and B$_6$

Carrots and bananas provide an astounding amount of vitamin B$_6$. From skin care to emotional disturbances due to hormone fluctuation (including PMS and menopause), the health benefits of B$_6$ stretch to include protection from heart disease and certain cancers.

Beet Booster

*Beets, beets, beets! This purple smoothie is not only attractive; it's also a delicious
way to sneak plenty of fruit and vegetable servings into your diet.*

INGREDIENTS | SERVES 2

1 cup beet greens

3 beets

1 frozen banana

2 cups water, divided

1. Place the beet greens, beets, banana, and 1 cup of water in a blender and blend until thoroughly combined.

2. Add the remaining water while blending until desired texture is achieved.

Calming Cucumber

The light taste of cucumber and the powerfully fragrant mint combine with the deep green romaine in this delightfully smooth and refreshing smoothie. Not only can this be a great start to your day, but it can also be the sweet end of it!

INGREDIENTS | SERVES 2

1 cup romaine lettuce

2 cucumbers, peeled and cut into chunks

¼ cup chopped mint

1 cup water, divided

1. Place the romaine, cucumbers, mint, and ½ cup water in a blender and combine thoroughly.

2. Add the remaining water while blending until desired texture is achieved.

Cucumbers Aren't Just Water

Even though a cucumber is mostly water (and fiber), it is far more than a tasty, hydrating, and filling snack option. These green veggies are a great addition to a diet in need of moisture and clarity . . . for the skin! A clear complexion is an aesthetic benefit of consuming cucumbers. By consuming 1 serving of cucumbers per day, not only will you get a full serving of veggies and stave off hunger, but you'll also have clear, hydrated skin!

CHAPTER 14

Beverages

Slow Cooker Spiced Cider

The aroma of this warming cider will fill your whole house!

1. Place the cinnamon sticks, ginger, and cloves into a cheesecloth packet. Place the packet, the cider, brown sugar, and nutmeg into a 6-quart slow cooker. Stir until the sugar dissolves.

2. Cook on high for 2–3 hours or until very hot. Reduce to low to keep hot until serving. Remove the packet after cooking if desired.

Make a Cheesecloth Packet

Place the items to be enclosed on a length of cheesecloth. Cut out a square about three times larger than the area the items take up. Pull all ends toward the middle and tie closed with kitchen twine.

Classic Hot Chocolate

This is the perfect drink for a cold winter morning.

1. In a large saucepan, whisk together the cocoa, sugar, and water over medium heat.

2. Add the milk and heat until warmed through. Serve with whipped cream or a marshmallow on top.

Vanilla Bean White Hot Chocolate

Children love this creamy, rich, warm vanilla-y drink made with white chocolate pieces.

INGREDIENTS | SERVES 8

8 cups whole milk

1 (12-ounce) package white chocolate chips

2 tablespoons vanilla extract

⅛ teaspoon salt

1 vanilla bean

2 cups whipped heavy cream

1. Add the milk, white chocolate chips, vanilla, and salt to a 4-quart stockpot. Use a whisk to combine the ingredients thoroughly.

2. Using a sharp knife, cut the vanilla bean in half and scrape out the tiny seeds and add them to the milk mixture.

3. Warm over medium-low heat, stirring occasionally, until warmed through. Serve in large mugs or coffee cups with whipped cream on top.

Peppermint Mocha Latte

A refreshing and festive coffee drink you can make right at home. You can also make a chilled Peppermint Mocha Latte by refrigerating the leftovers and serving the drink over ice the next day.

INGREDIENTS | SERVES 6

3 cups whole milk

3 cups strongly brewed coffee

¼ cup unsweetened cocoa

⅓ cup granulated sugar

½ teaspoon peppermint extract

⅛ teaspoon salt

2 cups whipped heavy cream

1. Add the milk, coffee, cocoa, sugar, peppermint extract, and salt to a large saucepan. Use a whisk to combine the ingredients thoroughly.

2. Warm over medium-low heat, stirring occasionally, until warmed through. Serve in large mugs or coffee cups with whipped cream on top.

Hot Caramel

If you're not a chocolate lover but you crave a warm, sweet drink on a cold morning, try this hot caramel!

INGREDIENTS | SERVES 4

⅔ cup Homemade Caramel Sauce (see sidebar)

4 cups whole milk

Fresh whipped cream (optional)

Mix the Homemade Caramel Sauce with the milk in a large saucepan. Heat over medium heat, stirring often. Serve hot with whipped cream on top, if desired, and a drizzle of extra caramel sauce.

How to Make Homemade Caramel Sauce

In a medium saucepan, combine ¼ cup water, 1¼ cups granulated sugar, and 2 tablespoons corn syrup. Cook undisturbed (do not stir after the initial combining of the ingredients) over medium-high heat for about 10 minutes. Every so often, swirl the pan but do not stir. The sauce will begin to turn amber. Swirl the sauce every 1–2 minutes for another 3–6 minutes or until it is a nice amber color. Carefully remove from the heat and quickly whisk in ⅓ cup heavy cream; be careful as the sauce can expand quickly. Stir in 2 tablespoons butter and ¼ teaspoon vanilla extract and let the sauce come to room temperature. This sauce keeps well in a sealed jar for 2 to 3 weeks in the refrigerator.

Maple Pumpkin Spice Latte

This warm latte is reminiscent of a drink you would pay big bucks for at a local coffee chain. By making your own you're not only saving money, but you'll have enough for a whole week's worth of breakfasts. Try it with a whipped cream topping.

INGREDIENTS | SERVES 8

2 cups brewed very strong coffee or espresso

4 cups whole milk

¾ cup plain pumpkin purée

⅓ cup maple syrup

1 tablespoon vanilla extract

2 teaspoons pumpkin pie spice

Place all the ingredients in a large saucepan and whisk to combine. Heat over medium-low heat, stirring occasionally, until warmed through. Serve immediately.

Make Your Own Pumpkin Pie Spice

If you don't have pumpkin pie spice, mix together 3 tablespoons ground cinnamon, 2 tablespoons ground ginger, 2 teaspoons ground nutmeg, 1½ teaspoons ground allspice, and 1½ teaspoons ground cloves. Store in an airtight container.

Salted Caramel Mocha Latte

The slight hint of salt in this warm, creamy drink balances out the sweetness of the caramel. When serving this sweet drink, offer whipped cream, additional caramel sauce, chocolate syrup, or sea salt for toppings.

INGREDIENTS | SERVES 6

3 cups whole milk

3 cups strongly brewed coffee

2 tablespoons unsweetened cocoa

⅓ cup granulated sugar

¼ teaspoon salt

1 teaspoon vanilla extract

⅓ cup caramel sauce

Place all the ingredients in a large saucepan and whisk to combine. Heat over medium-low heat, stirring occasionally, until warmed through. Top with whipped cream and serve in large mugs.

Strongly Brewed Coffee

To get a very strong coffee flavor in this drink, use about 3–4 tablespoons of ground coffee per cup of water. The coffee will be diluted when combined with the milk and will be creamy and delicious.

Iced Mocha

This frosty drink is just like the pricey ones you get at your local coffee shop, but you can make it at home and you don't even have to get out of your pajamas.

INGREDIENTS | SERVES 3–4

¼ cup unsweetened cocoa

¼ cup granulated sugar

2 cups whole milk

2 cups cold strongly brewed coffee, chilled

Coffee ice cubes

1. Place the cocoa and sugar in a blender and pulse a few times until thoroughly combined. Add the milk and coffee and blend on high for about 5–10 seconds or until the sugar is dissolved.

2. Serve over coffee ice cubes.

Coffee Ice Cubes

Pour your leftover morning coffee into ice cube trays and freeze so you have them available anytime you want to enjoy a cold coffee drink!

Mulled Cranberry Punch

The tart and sweet flavors of this punch simmered with warm spices make it a perfect drink to serve for a fall brunch.

INGREDIENTS | SERVES 10

1 (11.5-ounce) can frozen white grape–raspberry juice concentrate

1 (32-ounce) bottle cranberry juice

4 cups water

1 orange

2 cinnamon sticks, broken

8 whole cloves

4 whole allspice

No Cheesecloth?

Instead of using cheesecloth to create the spice bag in this mulled punch, you can simply use a large metal or plastic tea ball to place all the spices in while the tea is simmering. When you've finished using it, discard the spices and rinse out the tea ball to use again.

1. In a 4- to 6-quart slow cooker, combine the juice concentrate, cranberry juice, and water.

2. Using a vegetable peeler, remove a long peel from the orange. Juice the orange and strain out the seeds. Add the strained orange juice to the slow cooker.

3. Using a double-thickness square of cheesecloth, place the orange peel, cinnamon sticks, cloves, and allspice in the center. Close up the cheesecloth and tie up using kitchen string. Add the spice bag to the slow cooker.

4. Cover and cook on low for 6 hours or on high for 3 hours. Discard the spice bag and serve with the slow cooker turned to the warm setting.

Traditional Wassail

Submitted by Michelle Mayk. This version of the traditional holiday beverage is nonalcoholic so the kids can enjoy it too.

INGREDIENTS | SERVES 20

3 cinnamon sticks
1 tablespoon whole cloves
1 tablespoon whole allspice
1 gallon apple cider
1 large can unsweetened pineapple juice
½ cup orange juice
1 cup brewed herbal tea

1. Place the cinnamon sticks, cloves, and allspice in a cheesecloth, tie it off with kitchen string, and place it in a slow cooker.

2. Pour the cider, juices, and tea into a 4- or 6-quart slow cooker. Cover and simmer on low for 3–5 hours.

3. Remove the spice sack and serve warm.

Meaning of Wassailing

Wassail is Old English for "be you healthy." What once was a simple greeting became the beverage associated with an ancient English drinking ritual intended to ensure a good apple harvest the following year. Eventually it became part of our Christmas traditions. *Wassailing* refers to the habit of visiting neighbors, singing carols, and sharing drinks during the Yuletide season.

Classic Eggnog

Nothing says Christmas like a frothy glass of eggnog, but this delicious drink can (and should) be enjoyed year round! Serve it as a quick breakfast on a busy morning or as a luxurious beverage at your next brunch.

INGREDIENTS | SERVES 6

8 large eggs

⅓ cup pure maple syrup

4 teaspoons pure vanilla extract

2 cups whole milk

2 cups heavy cream

½ teaspoon ground nutmeg

½ teaspoon ground cinnamon

2 tablespoons granulated sugar

Cooking with Raw Eggs

If you choose to use raw eggs in this recipe, use only properly refrigerated, fresh, and clean grade A or AA eggs with intact shells. If desired, you can heat the milk and cream just to a boil and then temper the hot mixture into the eggs/syrup mixture before returning to the pot and heating to 160°F. Then add the vanilla, nutmeg, and cinnamon and fold in the egg whites; chill before serving.

1. Separate the egg yolks from the whites. Set the whites aside and place the yolks in a blender.

2. Add the syrup, vanilla, milk, cream, nutmeg, and cinnamon to the blender. Process until smooth. You can serve it at this point, or continue to the next step for a lighter, frothy eggnog.

3. In a mixing bowl, beat the egg whites until soft peaks form, then add the sugar and beat until stiff peaks form. Gently fold the egg whites into the eggnog with a rubber spatula. Chill until ready to serve.

4. Serve eggnog in small mugs with a sprinkle of freshly grated nutmeg if desired. Optional: Add 3–4 ounces bourbon for a festive holiday drink.

Pumpkin Eggnog

*This recipe takes eggnog to a whole new level. The pumpkin spice
flavor makes it perfect for your autumn gatherings.*

INGREDIENTS | SERVES 6

Classic Eggnog (see recipe in
this chapter)
½ cup canned pumpkin purée
¼ teaspoon ground allspice

Follow the Classic Eggnog instructions, but add the
pumpkin purée and allspice to the blender ingredients, and
reduce the vanilla extract to 1 teaspoon.

Nutella Eggnog

*If you thought pumpkin eggnog was decadent, wait until you try
Nutella eggnog! Moms, save this one for the weekends!*

INGREDIENTS | SERVES 6

8 egg yolks
2 cups whole milk
2 cups heavy cream
½ cup Nutella (or other hazelnut spread)
½ cup granulated sugar
Whipped cream for topping

Place all the ingredients except the whipped cream in a
blender. Process until smooth. Serve in small mugs with
whipped cream on top.

Slow Cooker Chai Tea

Feel free to leave the cardamom pods out of this warm tea if you don't have them readily available. Alternately, you can purchase ground cardamom and sprinkle a little on each serving of tea.

INGREDIENTS | SERVES 8

8 cups water

2 family-size black tea bags (or 8 individual-size tea bags)

½ cup granulated sugar

16 whole cloves

16 whole cardamom seeds, removed from pods

5 cinnamon sticks

2" knob ginger, peeled

1 cup 2% milk

1. Add the water, tea bags, sugar, cloves, cardamom, cinnamon sticks, and ginger to a 4-quart slow cooker.

2. Cover and cook on high for 3 hours or on low for 6 hours. Before serving, use a metal or plastic sieve to remove the spices, ginger, and tea bags from the tea.

3. Slowly stir in the milk and turn the slow cooker to the warm setting for serving. Leave the tea in the slow cooker for no more than 2 hours on the warm setting. The tea can be refrigerated and reheated for later use.

Easy Fruit Punch

This easy fruit punch is perfect for a holiday brunch. Kids love it, and you can easily kick it up a notch with your favorite spirit (try rum or gluten-free vodka) for an adult beverage.

INGREDIENTS | SERVES 10

1 liter Sprite or your favorite lemon-lime soda

4 cups cranberry juice cocktail

3 cups orange juice

Pour all the ingredients in a pitcher and stir. Serve over ice.

Mimosa

*No brunch is complete without a mimosa! This classic pairing
of champagne and orange juice is always a hit.*

INGREDIENTS | SERVES 6

1 bottle champagne or your favorite
sparkling wine, chilled

½ gallon orange juice, chilled

6 chilled champagne flutes

Fill each champagne flute halfway with champagne or sparkling wine. Top off with orange juice. Serve immediately. Optional: Add a splash of Triple Sec.

Fruity Pink Punch

*Submitted by Michelle Mayk. This fruity punch blends the flavors of pineapple, grape,
and cranberry with citrus to make a refreshing beverage for any time of year.*

INGREDIENTS | YIELDS 12 CUPS

3 cups pineapple juice

2 cups grape juice

2 quarts cranberry juice

6 ounces orange juice
concentrate, thawed

2½ cups lemon juice

1½ quarts chilled ginger ale

Pour all the ingredients in a pitcher and stir. Serve over ice.

Lime Sherbet Punch

This pretty pastel punch is perfect for bridal and brunch-time baby showers or wedding receptions.

INGREDIENTS | YIELDS 10 LITERS OR 2.5 GALLONS

1 gallon lime sherbet
2 (46-ounce) cans pineapple juice
3 liters chilled ginger ale

Spoon the sherbet into a large punch bowl. Pour the pineapple juice and ginger ale over the sherbet and stir carefully to blend until the sherbet stars to melt. Serve immediately.

Fruit and Spreads

Ultimate Fruit Salad

The citrusy sauce makes this traditional fruit salad come alive! Feel free to change up the fruit you include based on what's in season.

INGREDIENTS | SERVES 12

1 cup orange juice

½ cup lemon juice

⅓ cup honey

1 cup halved seedless green or red grapes

2 cups cubed mango

3 cups halved strawberries

3 kiwis, peeled and sliced

4 bananas, sliced

2 cups blueberries

1. Combine the orange juice, lemon juice, and honey in a saucepan. Bring to a boil over medium heat and then reduce heat and simmer for 5 minutes. Remove from heat and let cool.

2. Meanwhile, prepare the fruit and place it in a large clear bowl. Pour the cooled sauce over the fruit and gently stir to combine. Refrigerate for several hours to allow the flavors to soak in. Serve cold.

Mixed Berry Parfait

The layers of sweet fruit, tangy yogurt, and crunchy granola make a lovely light breakfast. Any combination of your favorite berries will work well in this recipe.

INGREDIENTS | SERVES 4

2 cups vanilla yogurt

2 cups gluten-free granola

2 cups blueberries, raspberries, and/or sliced strawberries

Whipped cream for topping, optional

In parfait dishes or wine glasses, layer the yogurt, granola, and berries. Repeat. Top with a dollop of whipped cream for a tasty garnish if desired.

Parfait: Something Perfect!

Parfait in French literally translated means "something perfect." Traditionally a dessert made with ice cream, more recently parfait has become a popular breakfast item when made with yogurt.

Apple Walnut Parfait

This nutty parfait makes a great addition to an autumn brunch menu.
Feel free to substitute granola for the walnuts if you prefer.

INGREDIENTS | SERVES 4

2 cups plain yogurt

¼ cup honey

1 cup coarsely chopped toasted walnuts

2 cups unsweetened applesauce

1 teaspoon ground cinnamon

1 cup raisins

In parfait dishes or wine glasses, create thin layers of yogurt, a drizzle of honey, walnuts, applesauce, a sprinkle of cinnamon, and raisins. Repeat. Top with a dollop of yogurt.

Apple Compote

Apple compote is fabulous over pancakes, waffles, or even French toast for a special breakfast treat.

INGREDIENTS | SERVES 4

8 sweet apples (such as Golden Delicious or McIntosh)

1 tablespoon butter

⅓ cup granulated sugar

½ teaspoon ground cinnamon

½ teaspoon vanilla extract

Peel, core, and slice the apples. Place them in a saucepan over medium heat. Melt the butter and add the sugar and cinnamon. Cook, stirring occasionally, until the apples are soft, about 25 minutes. Remove from heat and stir in the vanilla. Serve warm.

Caramelized Pear Parfait

This recipe comes courtesy of Melissa Angert, AllThingsChic.net. There are over three thousand varieties of pears grown around the world, but Bartlett and Anjou are most commonly found in American supermarkets. Either will work beautifully in this dish.

INGREDIENTS | SERVES 4–6

4 firm pears, cored and quartered
2 teaspoons fresh lemon juice
3 tablespoons butter
1 teaspoon ground cinnamon
⅛ teaspoon ground allspice
¼ cup light brown sugar (not packed)
1⅓ cups vanilla yogurt
1 cup gluten-free granola

1. Place the pears in a bowl, brush with lemon juice, and set aside.

2. Heat a large skillet over high heat. Add the butter and the pears and cook for 3–4 minutes, stirring occasionally, until golden brown around the edges.

3. Add the cinnamon and allspice and toss gently to combine. Add the brown sugar and cook for 2–3 more minutes, stirring occasionally until the pears are soft and the juices have blended with the sugar to form a syrup.

4. Assemble the parfaits by layering yogurt, pears, and granola. Top with a drizzle of leftover syrup from the pan. Parfaits may be assembled while pears are warm or after they have cooled.

Citrus Compote

*Compote gets better with age, so feel free to make it the day before,
and then just spoon it over a bowl of yogurt for breakfast.*

INGREDIENTS | SERVES 4

2 oranges

2 grapefruits

4 mandarin oranges

½ cup granulated sugar

1 vanilla bean

What Is Compote?

Compote originated in seventeenth-century France. It is made by cooking fruit in water with sugar and spices. You can serve compote over yogurt or pancakes for a breakfast treat or serve it over ice cream for a decadent dessert. Compote can also be frozen in canning jars, making it a great way to use up ripe fruit.

1. Zest 1 orange and put the zest in a medium saucepan. Peel and section the oranges, grapefruit, and mandarin oranges and place in a bowl, adding their juice to the saucepan. Split the vanilla bean pod and scrape out the seeds into the saucepan (reserve the pod).

2. Heat the juice (it should be approximately ½ cup; add water if necessary) with the orange zest, sugar, vanilla seeds, and pod until boiling. Stir until the sugar dissolves, then reduce heat and simmer for 2 minutes. Remove from heat and allow to cool.

3. Discard the vanilla pod and toss the syrup with reserved fruit. Serve over yogurt for a light breakfast.

Baked Pear Crumble

Pears are a lovely fall fruit and often get overlooked because they share their season with the popular apple. These baked pears topped with yogurt and a crunchy, nutty streusel topping make a wonderful autumn breakfast dish.

INGREDIENTS | SERVES 4

2 Anjou pears, peeled and cut in half lengthwise

3 tablespoons melted butter, divided

½ cup chopped pecans

¼ cup pumpkin seeds

¼ packed cup light brown sugar

2 tablespoons gluten-free old-fashioned rolled oats

½ teaspoon ground cinnamon

¼ teaspoon salt

1 cup vanilla yogurt

Anjou Pears

Anjou pears have a mild flavor and a firm texture, while still being sweet and juicy. Bosc pears also work well in this dish.

1. Preheat oven to 350°F. Place the pears, cut-side up, on a small baking sheet and brush with 1 tablespoon melted butter. Bake on an upper rack until soft, 25–30 minutes. Allow to cool.

2. Meanwhile, combine the remaining 2 tablespoons butter, pecans, pumpkin seeds, brown sugar, oats, cinnamon, and salt and spread on a baking sheet. Roast on a lower rack until golden brown, 12–15 minutes. Give the pan a good shake about halfway through so it browns evenly. Allow to cool.

3. Serve the pears topped with a dollop of vanilla yogurt and the crumble topping.

Fruit Pizza

Serve this fruit pizza at your next brunch, and you will have some happy houseguests! The secret is to underbake the cookie dough just a bit so that it is soft and doughy.

INGREDIENTS | SERVES 8

1 bag gluten-free sugar cookie mix such as Bob's Red Mill Shortbread Cookie Mix

12 ounces cream cheese, room temperature

½ cup butter, room temperature

1 teaspoon pure vanilla extract

2 cups powdered sugar

Assorted fresh fruit (such as strawberries, kiwi, grapes, blueberries, and peaches)

1. Prepare the cookie dough according to package directions; chill in the refrigerator for several hours.

2. Preheat oven to 350°F. Roll out the cookie dough to fill a round baking sheet. This is your "pizza crust." Bake for 15–20 minutes or until set, but not yet starting to brown; you don't want it to be quite cooked through. Chill in the refrigerator.

3. Mix together the cream cheese, butter, vanilla, and sugar in a bowl; spread the frosting on the chilled cookie. Return to the refrigerator to set the frosting.

4. Meanwhile, prepare the fruit. Wash and slice or cube to make them easy to place on the cookie.

5. Arrange the fruit on the pizza and serve!

Cinnamon Maple Bread Stuffed Apples

This recipe comes from Karla Walsh, HealthfulBitesBlog.com. Apple pie is delicious, but who has time to slave over the cutting board and oven on a busy weekday? Enter the baked apple! This decadent, single-serve dessert can be made in no time.

INGREDIENTS | SERVES 6

2 tablespoons peanut flour
¼ teaspoon baking powder
⅛ teaspoon baking soda
¼ teaspoon ground cinnamon
1 teaspoon stevia
1 tablespoon unsweetened applesauce
½ teaspoon egg white
¼ teaspoon maple extract
1 medium apple
¼ teaspoon lemon juice
Vanilla Greek yogurt and more cinnamon for serving (optional)

1. Preheat oven to 350°F and fill a glass 13" × 9" baking dish with 1 tablespoon of water.

2. Combine the peanut flour, baking powder, baking soda, cinnamon, and stevia in a large mixing bowl.

3. Add the applesauce, egg white, and maple extract; stir to combine the wet and dry ingredients.

4. Remove the core from the apple and sprinkle the lemon juice on the inside to prevent browning. Place the cored apple in the prepared dish and pour the bread batter in the middle of the apple.

5. Bake for 25 minutes or until the bread is baked and the apple is tender. Serve with yogurt and an extra sprinkle of cinnamon, if desired.

Peach Marmalade

You can spread this marmalade on a fruit dish or try it on any of the breads in Chapter 7.

INGREDIENTS | YIELDS 8 CUPS

2 pounds peaches, peeled, pitted, and chopped

½ cup (about 6 ounces) dried apricots, chopped

1 (20-ounce) can pineapple tidbits in unsweetened juice, undrained

2 medium oranges

1 small lemon

2 cups honey

2 (3") cinnamon sticks

Innovative Peach Marmalade Uses

By keeping this marmalade the consistency of applesauce you have the added versatility of using it as a condiment on top of cooked chicken breasts, easily mixing it with a barbecue or chili sauce (gluten-free, of course) to create a sweet and savory dipping sauce, or using it to replace applesauce in many different recipes.

1. Add the peaches to a food processor or blender along with the apricots and pineapple (with juice).

2. Zest the oranges and lemon and add it to the food processor or blender. Cut the oranges and the lemon into quarters and remove any seeds, then add to the food processor or blender. Pulse until the entire fruit mixture is pulverized. Pour into a greased 4- to 6-quart slow cooker.

3. Add the honey to the slow cooker and stir to combine with the fruit mixture. Add the cinnamon sticks. Cover and, stirring occasionally, cook on low for 4 hours or until the mixture reaches the consistency of applesauce. When finished cooking, remove the cinnamon sticks.

4. Unless you process and seal the marmalade into sterilized jars, store in covered glass jars in the refrigerator for up to 3–4 weeks. The marmalade can also be frozen for up to 6 months.

Apple Butter

Depending on when you start this recipe, it can take up to 2 days to complete, but it is great for spreading on gluten-free toast for brunch.

INGREDIENTS | YIELDS 5 CUPS

6 apples, peeled, cored, and quartered
½ tablespoon vanilla extract
⅔ cup honey
1 teaspoon ground cinnamon
¼ teaspoon ground cloves

1. Place the apples and vanilla extract in a 4- to 6-quart slow cooker. Cover and cook on low for 8 hours.

2. Mash the apples with a fork. Stir in the honey, cinnamon, and cloves.

3. Cover and cook on low for 6 hours. Allow to cool at room temperature or in the refrigerator for 1–2 hours. Serve chilled or at room temperature.

Blackberry Jam

This easy low-sugar jam does not need to be canned; it will keep up to a month in the refrigerator.

INGREDIENTS | YIELDS 1 QUART

3 cups fresh blackberries
1¾ ounces no-sugar pectin
½ cup honey
¾ cup water

1. Place all the ingredients in a 2-quart slow cooker. Stir.

2. Cook on high, uncovered, for 5 hours. Using a fork or potato masher, smash the berries a bit until they are the texture you prefer. Pour the jam into an airtight container.

3. Refrigerate overnight before using.

Strawberry Jelly

Together with almond butter, they make the perfect pair—"AB and J" (almond butter and jelly).

INGREDIENTS | SERVES 24

1½ quarts ripe strawberries, washed and hulled

3¾ cups honey

¼ cup lemon juice

1. Place the strawberries in a 4-quart slow cooker. Stir in the honey and lemon juice. Cover and cook on high for 2½ hours, stirring twice.

2. Uncover and continue cooking for 2 more hours or until the preserves have thickened, stirring occasionally.

3. Ladle into hot, sterilized ½-pint jelly jars, seal, and store in the refrigerator for up to 2 weeks.

Cinnamon Fruit Dip

This recipe was submitted by Mary Carver, GivingUpOnPerfect.com.
This dip is perfect for serving with fruit for brunch.

INGREDIENTS | MAKES 2 CUPS

7 ounces gluten-free marshmallow crème such as Kraft

8 ounces cream cheese, softened

½ cup powdered sugar

1 teaspoon pure vanilla extract

½ teaspoon ground cinnamon

Add all the ingredients to a bowl and stir to combine. Serve with fruit.

Pear Butter

*Enjoy pear season, all year long! Drizzle over some fresh fruit salad
for a sweet addition to a traditional breakfast favorite.*

INGREDIENTS | SERVES 8

8 pears of any variety, peeled, cored, and sliced

2 cups water

¾ cup honey

Juice of 1 lemon

1 whole star anise

¼ teaspoon ground ginger

¼ teaspoon ground nutmeg

1. Place all the ingredients in a 6-quart slow cooker, cover, and cook on low for 10–12 hours.

2. Uncover and cook on low for an additional 10–12 hours, until thick and most of the liquid has been absorbed.

3. Allow to cool and remove the star anise before puréeing in a blender. Store in airtight canning jars.

Apricot Butter

Makes a tasteful substitute for orange marmalade.

INGREDIENTS | SERVES 8

5 ripe apricots, washed, peeled, pitted, and puréed in food processor

1½ cups honey

2 teaspoons ground cinnamon

1 teaspoon ground cloves

1½ tablespoons lemon juice

1. Pour the puréed apricots into a 4- to 6-quart slow cooker and add the honey, spices, and lemon juice. Mix well.

2. Cover and cook on high for 8–10 hours, until thick. Remove the cover halfway through cooking. Stir periodically.

3. Store in refrigerator, in an airtight canning jar, or freeze.

Blueberry Butter Bliss

A blueberry lover's dream. This antioxidant-rich spread proves blueberries do live up to their often referred to nickname, a superfood!

INGREDIENTS | SERVES 7

4 cups fresh blueberries, puréed
¾ cup honey
½ lemon zest
1 teaspoon ground cinnamon
¼ teaspoon grated nutmeg

1. Pour the puréed blueberries into a 4- to 6-quart slow cooker and cover. Cook on low for 5 hours.

2. Remove the lid and add the honey, lemon zest, and spices, mixing well. Turn heat to high and cook for 1 more hour, uncovered.

3. Once the butter is cooked down sufficiently, pour into canning jars and cover tightly.

4. Process canning jars in boiling water for 10 minutes. Store unopened jars in a cool, dark place.

Fig Jam

A versatile spread sure to liven up any breakfast sweet bread, and is loaded with fiber and phytonutrients.

INGREDIENTS | SERVES 3 (½ CUP SERVINGS)

2 pounds fresh figs, peeled and cut into eighths
1 cup honey
½ cup water
1 lemon, diced, including the rind, seeds removed
3 tablespoons finely diced crystallized ginger

1. Add all the ingredients to a 2- to 3-quart slow cooker. Cover and cook on high for 4 hours.

2. Remove the cover and cook for an additional 1–2 hours, until the mixture reaches a jam-like consistency.

3. While still hot, pour into clean, sterilized 4-ounce jars and store covered in the refrigerator for up to 3 weeks.

Cranberry Honey Butter

This recipe comes from Stacie Connerty, TheDivineMissMommy.com. This spread is perfect on biscuits or toast. It also makes a great hostess gift. It whips together in no time and keeps in the refrigerator for about 2 weeks.

INGREDIENTS | YIELDS 2 CUPS

1 cup soft butter

1 cup whole cranberry sauce

¼ cup honey

¼ teaspoon sea salt

Using the paddle attachment of an electric mixer, combine all the ingredients. Whip together until fully incorporated, about 2 minutes. Scoop into a glass jar.

Orange Chia Pudding Parfait

This recipe was submitted by Noelle Kelly, SingersKitchen.com. This dish is filling and tasty and super quick to make.

INGREDIENTS | SERVES 2

¼ cup chia seeds

2 cups fresh orange or tangerine juice

2 tablespoons agave nectar or maple syrup

1½ bananas, sliced

1 cup sliced fresh strawberries

1. Place the chia seeds, orange juice, and agave in a medium bowl and stir to combine. Allow the mixture to sit for 10 minutes, periodically stirring so that all the seeds absorb the juice.

2. Add ¼ cup of the orange chia pudding to the bottom of each of 2 parfait glasses, then add some of the bananas and strawberries. Repeat with more pudding and repeat the process again until finishing with pudding. Decorate with fruit and eat.

Slow-Roasted Pineapple

This recipe is courtesy of Colleen Kennedy, SouffleBombay.com. Roasting a pineapple brings out its syrupy sweetness and turns this already delicious fruit into a decadent treat!

INGREDIENTS | SERVES 4

1 whole pineapple

1. Preheat oven to 325°F.

2. Slice off the leafy green top of the pineapple, cutting just to where it ends. Place the pineapple standing up on a baking sheet and roast for 1 hour (if it is a super-large pineapple, add 15 minutes).

3. Turn off the oven, leave the door closed, and allow the pineapple to cool in the oven for 1 more hour.

4. After 1 hour of cooling, slice off the top and the bottom. Cut off the skin and the eyes. Slice into rounds and eat around the core or core the slices and serve the halves.

APPENDIX A

Websites for Gluten-Free Support

National Foundation for Celiac Awareness

A comprehensive resource for gluten-free information, recipes, resources, and more.
www.celiaccentral.org

Celiac.com

A gluten-free forum with an active community where you can post questions and comments on various gluten-free related topics.
www.Celiac.com

Gluten Free Living

A website by *Gluten-Free Living* magazine with interactive features, articles, news and current events, recipes, advice, tips, and more.
www.glutenfreeliving.com

Gluten-Free Girl

A blog written by Shauna James Ahern with gluten-free recipes, cooking videos, a guide to gluten-free baking, and personal anecdotes about living and thriving on the gluten-free lifestyle.
www.glutenfreegirl.com

Gluten Free on a Shoestring

A blog with gluten-free recipes and resources and how to live gluten-free on a budget.
www.glutenfreeonashoestring.com

Elana's Pantry

A blog by Elana Amsterdam, a pioneer in grain-free cooking and baking and author of the *New York Times* Best Selling cookbook *Paleo Cooking from Elana's Pantry*.
www.elanaspantry.com

Celiac Chicks

A gluten-free blog focusing primarily on product reviews and travel and restaurant reviews.
www.celiacchicks.com

Gluten Free Easy

A resource for up-to-date information on gluten-free living and gluten-free products.
www.glutenfreeeasy.com

Udi's Gluten Free Community

An online community run by Udi's, a popular gluten-free foods brand, where you can ask questions and get advice about gluten-free living.
www.udisglutenfree.com/community

Pamela's Products

The official site for Pamela's Products, this site also includes recipes, how-to videos, baking tips, and allergy information.
www.pamelasproducts.com

Gluten Free Travel Site

An extensive database of user-submitted restaurant and travel reviews for the gluten-free lifestyle.
www.glutenfreetravelsite.com

Standard U.S./Metric Measurement Conversions

VOLUME CONVERSIONS

U.S. Volume Measure	Metric Equivalent
⅛ teaspoon	0.5 milliliter
¼ teaspoon	1 milliliter
½ teaspoon	2 milliliters
1 teaspoon	5 milliliters
½ tablespoon	7 milliliters
1 tablespoon (3 teaspoons)	15 milliliters
2 tablespoons (1 fluid ounce)	30 milliliters
¼ cup (4 tablespoons)	60 milliliters
⅓ cup	90 milliliters
½ cup (4 fluid ounces)	125 milliliters
⅔ cup	160 milliliters
¾ cup (6 fluid ounces)	180 milliliters
1 cup (16 tablespoons)	250 milliliters
1 pint (2 cups)	500 milliliters
1 quart (4 cups)	1 liter (about)

WEIGHT CONVERSIONS

U.S. Weight Measure	Metric Equivalent
½ ounce	15 grams
1 ounce	30 grams
2 ounces	60 grams
3 ounces	85 grams
¼ pound (4 ounces)	115 grams
½ pound (8 ounces)	225 grams
¾ pound (12 ounces)	340 grams
1 pound (16 ounces)	454 grams

OVEN TEMPERATURE CONVERSIONS

Degrees Fahrenheit	Degrees Celsius
200 degrees F	95 degrees C
250 degrees F	120 degrees C
275 degrees F	135 degrees C
300 degrees F	150 degrees C
325 degrees F	160 degrees C
350 degrees F	180 degrees C
375 degrees F	190 degrees C
400 degrees F	205 degrees C
425 degrees F	220 degrees C
450 degrees F	230 degrees C

BAKING PAN SIZES

U.S.	Metric
8 × 1½ inch round baking pan	20 × 4 cm cake tin
9 × 1½ inch round baking pan	23 × 3.5 cm cake tin
11 × 7 × 1½ inch baking pan	28 × 18 × 4 cm baking tin
13 × 9 × 2 inch baking pan	30 × 20 × 5 cm baking tin
2 quart rectangular baking dish	30 × 20 × 3 cm baking tin
15 × 10 × 2 inch baking pan	30 × 25 × 2 cm baking tin (Swiss roll tin)
9 inch pie plate	22 × 4 or 23 × 4 cm pie plate
7 or 8 inch springform pan	18 or 20 cm springform or loose-bottom cake tin
9 × 5 × 3 inch loaf pan	23 × 13 × 7 cm or 2 lb narrow loaf or pâté tin
1½ quart casserole	1.5 liter casserole
2 quart casserole	2 liter casserole

Index

We Have

EVERYTHING®

on Anything!

With more than 19 million copies sold, the Everything® series has become one of America's favorite resources for solving problems, learning new skills, and organizing lives. Our brand is not only recognizable—it's also welcomed.

The series is a hand-in-hand partner for people who are ready to tackle new subjects—like you!

For more information on the Everything® series, please visit *www.adamsmedia.com*

The Everything® list spans a wide range of subjects, with more than 500 titles covering 25 different categories:

Business	History	Reference
Careers	Home Improvement	Religion
Children's Storybooks	Everything Kids	Self-Help
Computers	Languages	Sports & Fitness
Cooking	Music	Travel
Crafts and Hobbies	New Age	Wedding
Education/Schools	Parenting	Writing
Games and Puzzles	Personal Finance	
Health	Pets	